W9-CBH-279

Twayne's English Authors Series

Sylvia E. Bowman, *Editor*

INDIANA UNIVERSITY

Arthur Machen

TEAS 8

Arthur Machen

By WESLEY D. SWEETSER
University of Nebraska

Twayne Publishers, Inc. :: New York

Library of Congress Catalog Card Number: 64-19033

MANUFACTURED IN THE UNITED STATES OF AMERICA

To Adrian Goldstone *and* Edwin Steffe

Preface

Though the primary emphasis in Twayne's English Authors Series is upon critical evaluation, I have taken the liberty of inserting more biographical data than is directly pertinent to the works themselves for two reasons. First, with such a relatively unknown author as Arthur Machen more background material must be given to place him in the proper perspective than would be necessary for a more famous literary figure. Second, Machen published his own life in *Far Off Things* and in *Things Near & Far;* but, for reasons of his own, he deliberately obscured certain facts and altered names and places. Furthermore, Machen's account ends with 1921 although he did not die until 1947. My study, therefore, attempts to remedy these deficiencies without, at the same time, neglecting the more serious consideration of the works themselves.

For those interested in bibliography, Adrian Goldstone and I have compiled a study of several hundred pages which describes all first editions in detail and which lists all the periodical contributions that we could locate. Of necessity, I have listed only a few of the periodicals for which Machen wrote and inclusive dates by year. Secondary sources have naturally been limited to the most important of several hundred possible entries.

W. D. S.

University of Nebraska
April, 1964

Contents

Chronology

1863 Arthur Machen born at Caerleon-on-Usk, Wales, March 3.
1874–1880 Attended Hereford Cathedral School.
1880 Failed examination for Royal College of Surgeons in London. Composed *Eleusinia.*
1881 Publication: *Eleusinia.*
1883 Worked as tutor, living at Clarendon Road, London. Composed *The Anatomy of Tobacco.*
1884 Publication: *The Anatomy of Tobacco.*
1884–1885 Composed *The Chronicle of Clemendy.*
1884–1888 Worked for publishers, notably George Redway, in London as a translator, editor, proofreader, and cataloger. Translated *The Heptameron,* 1884-1885.
1885 Mother died, November 10.
1886 Publication: *The Heptameron.*
1887 Married Amelia Hogg, August 31. Father died, September 29. Received inheritance sufficient to provide economic independence for the next fourteen years.
1888 Publication: *The Chronicle of Clemendy.*
1888–1889 Translated *The Memoirs of Jacques Casanova* and de Verville's *Le Moyen de Parvenir.*
1890 Formed casual acquaintance with Oscar Wilde which lasted for five years. Publication: *Fantastic Tales.*
1890–1891 Composed *The Great God Pan.*
1890–1894 Composed *The Three Impostors.*
1894 Publications: *The Great God Pan and the Inmost Light, The Memoirs of Jacques Casanova.*

1895 Composed *The Garden of Avallaunius* (*The Hill of Dreams*), 1895-1897. Publication: *The Three Impostors.*
1897 Composed *Ornaments in Jade.*
1898–1899 Worked as assistant editor and reviewer for *Literature* magazine.
1899 Amelia Machen died, July 31. Composed "The White People," *Hieroglyphics,* and part of *A Fragment of Life.*
1900 Joined Hermetic Order of the Golden Dawn.
1901–1909 Acted with the Benson Shakespeare Repertory Company and others.
1902 Publication: *Hieroglyphics.*
1903 Married Dorothie Purefoy Hudleston on June 25.
1904 Publication: *The House of the Hidden Light.*
1906 Composed *Dr. Stiggins.* Publications: *The House of Souls, Dr. Stiggins.*
1907 Wrote for *The Academy* magazine, 1907-1908. Composed *The Secret Glory.* Publication: *The Hill of Dreams.*
1908–1910 Wrote articles for *T.P.'s Weekly* later published as *Notes and Queries.*
1910–1921 Star reporter for *The Evening News.*
1914 Composed "The Bowmen."
1915 Composed *Far Off Things* and *The Great Return.* Publications: *The Angels of Mons, The Great Return.*
1916 Composed *The Terror.*
1917 Composed *War and the Christian Faith.* Publication: *The Terror.*
1918 Publication: *War and the Christian Faith.*
1919–1927 Lived the life of a semi-retired literary celebrity at St. John's Wood, London. Composed *Strange Roads, Dog and Duck, Things Near & Far, Dreads and Drolls,* and *The Canning Wonder.*
1922 Publications: *The Secret Glory, Far Off Things.*
1923 Publications: *Things Near & Far, The Shining Pyramid* (Covici-McGee), *Strange Roads.*
1924 Publications: *Dog and Duck, The London Adventure, The Glorious Mystery, Precious Balms, Ornaments in Jade, The Shining Pyramid* (Secker).
1925 Publication: *The Canning Wonder.*
1926 Publications: *Dreads and Drolls, Notes and Queries.*

1927–
1929 Lived at 28 Loudoun Road in great poverty.
1928 Received financial assistance from Robert Hillyer for three years.
1929 Moved to Old Amersham, Buckinghamshire, where he spent the remainder of his life.
1930 Publication: *Tom O'Bedlam and His Song.*
1931–
1934 Composed *Bridles & Spurs.*
1932 Received civil list pension of £100 per annum from King George V. Composed *The Green Round.* Publication: *A Few Letters from Arthur Machen.*
1933 Publication: *The Green Round.*
1935 Composed *Children of the Pool.*
1936 Publications: *The Cosy Room, The Children of the Pool.*
1938 Pension increased to £140.
1947 Purefoy Machen died, March 30. Arthur Machen died, December 15.
1951 Publication: *Bridles & Spurs.*

Arthur Machen

CHAPTER 1

He Dreamed in Fire

ARTHUR MACHEN'S position in the history of English literature has long been an enigma. His name appears in such varied studies as Wagenknecht's *Cavalcade of the English Novel,* Scarborough's *The Supernatural in Modern English Fiction,* Summers' *Witchcraft and Black Magic,* Waite's *The Holy Grail: Its Legends and Symbolism,* Praz's *The Romantic Agony,* Varma's *The Gothic Flame,* Mason's *Sir George Alexander & the St. James' Theatre,* Jackson's *The Eighteen Nineties,* and Cazamian's *L'Anti-Intellectualisme et L'Esthétisme: 1880-1900.* These titles suggest both the problem and the approach.

First of all, Machen achieved fame in no one field. Unlike Dickens, he is not known primarily as a novelist; unlike Lamb, as an essayist; unlike Algernon Blackwood, as a specialist in horror; unlike Cervantes or Rabelais, as the author of a single work. On the contrary, Machen's works range from outright translations to sheer fantasy, from horror to the supernatural, from the occult and esoteric to dogmatic assertions of opinion, from hack work to highly original creations. They are written in almost every literary form except drama and are composed in a variety of styles. One cause, therefore, of previous deficiencies in scholarship is the vast range and heterogeneity of his work.

Another aspect of the same problem arises from his long life span from the Victorian era to post-World War II. Thus he could conceivably be considered as a product of either of these two periods or of any one intervening. To further complicate the issue, his major works were written in the 1890's, but many of them were not published until later; and not until the 1920's, when his works were published en masse, did these earlier efforts receive any recognition.

In preference to piecing together a montage, the solution to unifying these disparate elements lies rather in placing the works in perspective: in considering them in relation to the events of his life and to the periods through which he lived. In this manner the general nature and pattern of his work can be considered while, at the same time, the *juvenilia,* the ephemerae, the purely commercial endeavors, and the imperfect specimens of his art can be eliminated from further consideration.

I *The Fort of the Legion*

Born on March 3, 1863, at Caerleon-on-Usk, Arthur Llewelyn Jones spent his early years at the nearby rectory at Llanddewi, where he lived as an only child. In a home consisting of an invalid mother, a clergyman father, brought up by a maiden aunt, he soon became inured to loneliness. He found solace in nature and in books.

Figuratively speaking, he was the product of the union between the Little People and the Roman Legion in the mystic region of Avalon. When his eyes "first opened in earliest childhood they had before them the vision of an enchanted land."[1] Caerleon, in the medieval district of Gwent, now Monmouthshire in the borderland of Wales, has, indeed, a certain magic in the surrounding heavily wooded, domed hills and in the silvery esses that feed into the spirituous Usk; but it has an even greater enchantment in the richness of its history. Archeological evidences of the early Roman occupation are still extant, these being one of the few "villas" in Wales and an amphitheater.

To the youthful Arthur these relics of ancient civilization were visible realities; and to him history was not a series of disjointed events, but a steady flow, merging the past with the present. Here, too, was the land of the mythical King Arthur and his Knights of the Round Table and the bastion of Christianity against the Nordic invaders, the point of fusion of legend and fact, of the story of Joseph of Arimethaea and the account of Bran the Blessed. Then history took precedence once more and left its mark in medieval abbeys, castles, and, finally, manor houses. Such was the imaginatively stimulating aura of old Isca in the land of the Silures.

At the same time that these environmental influences were making their mark, young Arthur was compensating for his lack of companionship by keeping company with some of the authors in his father's library. He read Cervantes, Dickens, De Quincey, Scott, Tennyson, the Brontës, and others. This solitary process of self-education constituted most of his early schooling, but many of the masterworks, particularly *Don Quixote* and *The Pickwick Papers,* remained favorites for the rest of his life.

In 1874, he began his formal schooling at Hereford Cathedral School, which dates back to the fourteenth century and which offers a sound classical education. Either because of his sense of alienation from other children or because of his father's lack of funds, he quit school from December, 1875, until midsummer, 1876. In 1874, his father had assumed the name Jones-Machen, the latter from the mother's side, probably in the hope of receiving an endowment for his son's education. When Arthur returned to Hereford, the name Jones-Machen appeared in *The Herefordian* toward the top of the class in both classics and divinity for several years.[2] Despite his intellectual success, however, Arthur Jones-Machen acquired no fondness for athletics or for the public school system in general. In April, 1880, he left in a spirit of revolt, taking with him a solid knowledge of French, Latin, and religion. He was reading the *Odyssey* at the time.

In Machen's case, all of these childhood impressions and recollections, all of the knowledge that he had gleaned formed the substratum for his literary career. Retrospectively, his own interpretation was: "What I had been doing was this: I had been inventing tales in which and by which I had tried to realize my boyish impressions of that wonderful magic Gwent."[3]

Indirectly, his first trip to London in July, 1880, to take the examination for the Royal College of Surgeons prompted his early creative efforts. Instead of pursuing the study of mathematics, as he was supposed to, he wrote juvenile verse of an artificial and heroic nature, incited by reading Swinburne's *Songs Before Sunrise.* As a consequence, he failed the examination and was compelled to return to Llanddewi for eight or nine months.[4] There he continued to work on his poetry until he had produced *Eleusinia,* published in one hundred copies at his own expense.[5] According to his own testimony, he simply turned an article in Smith's *Classical Dictionary* into verse—some blank, some rhymed, but all bad.[6]

Although not a noteworthy poetic achievement, this poem reveals his early interest in the mysteries. As applied to the poem the term "mysteries" is used in its most ancient sense. The subject is the secret rite surrounding the worship of Demeter in which only the initiated participate—"Now to the sea the mystai bend their steps. . . ." [7] The atmosphere is one of fervent rapture and adoration as the solemn procession winds slowly along; and the climax comes as a sudden light is seen, rather too obviously signifying revelation. With considerable insight into the past, Machen imbues this pagan rite with the feeling of awe and wonder which surrounded the worship of the invisible forces of nature before religion became so formalized as to lose its vital meaning. Years later, he explained his purpose in general terms: "For literature, as I see it, is the art of describing the indescribable; the art of exhibiting symbols which may hint at the ineffable mysteries behind them; the art of the veil, which reveals what it conceals." [8]

For a brief time he imitated William Morris and Robert Herrick, but he destroyed the results. Later in life, he apparently destroyed all but two copies of *Eleusinia* as well, thus making it a rare collector's item. Throughout his lifetime only three other poems were ever published—all short, insignificant, and unpoetic. Fortunately he realized his limitations and abandoned the medium. He never really understood scansion or prosody,[9] despite the subconscious rhythms later found in some of his prose.

The next three years—from June, 1881, to July, 1884—he spent in London, at first ostensibly studying shorthand in preparation for a journalistic career and later eking out a precarious subsistence by tutoring small children. For nearly two of these years, he stayed in a small cubicle at 23 Clarendon Road, where he endured extreme poverty—"*Peine forte et dure*" [10]—living on green tea and black tobacco. His way of life provided him with no sense of intellectual achievement, and he felt so ill-placed that he described himself as "a peg of no particular shape at all in a perfectly round hole. . . ." [11] If he had not aped Robert Burton and created a book called *The Anatomy of Tobacco,* he might well have gone mad from the combined effects of loneliness, hunger, and despair. The book was published by George Redway in 1884 at Machen's expense and after he returned to Gwent.

The Anatomy of Tobacco: or Smoking Methodized, Divided & Considered after a New Fashion, by Leolinus Siluriensis, Professor of Fumifical Philosophy in the University of Brentford, was a self-imposed task to enable Machen to escape from the prison of himself.[12] The book contains elements of Latin and Greek, scholastic logic, and a thin philosophy obtained from Wilhelm Gottlieb Tennemann's *A Manual of the History of Philosophy.*[13] The similarities to Burton's *Anatomy* are both self-acknowledged and obvious. The same copia, amplification, Latin and Greek tags, quotation from authority (occasionally fictitious), and the same learned disquisitions in high-flown diction, ending in a colloquialism, are present in both. To match Burton's "one must needs scratch where it itches" [14] is found Machen's "Mind your 'P's' and 'Q's'." [15] Both works have their witty and amusing side, though Machen's book is more limited and trivial in scope.

Although *The Anatomy of Tobacco* is a superficial and imitative work, it does reveal, toward the end, the embryonic development of Machen's attitude toward life. After attacking chewers and snuffers as gross materialists, he concludes by saying that the virtue of smoking exists in the mind of the smoker.[16] Even at that early date he was repudiating materialism. Already he had embraced the philosophy of idealism. Furthermore, four traits in common with Romantic writers are apparent: the element of wonder in common things, which Machen attributed to this work in retrospect;[17] withdrawal or escape from reality; the reverence for seventeenth-century authors and style; and the return to the medieval, in this case medieval scholasticism.

As a result of his correspondence with Redway concerning the publication of *The Anatomy,* Machen was commissioned to translate *The Heptameron* of Marguerite, Queen of Navarre for the sum of £20. Here, again, though the original is of an earlier period, he used the style of the Caroline age, this time a composite of Herrick, Taylor, Browne, Pepys, Fuller, and Walton. *The Heptameron* is patterned after Boccaccio's *Decameron,* the stories being linked together only by a traveler's device in the manner of Chaucer's *Canterbury Tales,* each tale having a professed moral. Cuckoldry, rape, lechery, and the carnal exploits of monks are the themes; and, in that respect, the tales are not unlike the medieval fabliau, except that the grosser and rowdier elements are lacking.

Machen started *The Chronicle of Clemendy* in 1885 at his old lodgings, 23 Clarendon Road. He was working for Redway at a salary of £60 per year cataloging rare books and compiling books of oddments,[18] like *The Literature of Occultism and Archaeology,* and acting as reader on novels submitted for publication. His stay in London was cut short, however, by word that his mother was dying. After her death he stayed on at Llanddewi for a year and completed *The Chronicle* by August, 1886.

Having been so recently in his mind, *The Heptameron* undoubtedly represents a primary stimulus in the creation of these medieval tales. *The Chronicle* resembles its source in three respects: first, in the use of the journey device; second, in the erotic nature of many of the tales; and, third, in the archaic, seventeenth-century style. According to Machen's own testimony, however, the origins of the impulse to write the book came from delight in Balzac's *Contes Drolatiques,* in Rabelais, and in Gwent. Machen's book was to be a voyage in search of the Oracle of the Holy Bottle, a great romance called *The Glory of Gwent;* but in his search for a medium, the dream was lost.[19]

Still, despite the extensive use of place names, nature description, and Welsh legend, the work is more than just local color; and despite the literary echoes of Burton, Malory, and Rabelais, it is not simply a feeble imitation. On the whole, the plots of the tales are indisputably original, and few elements are introduced to detract from the authenticity of the medieval setting. On the other hand, *The Chronicle* certainly does not approximate Octave Uzanne's claims for it in *Le Livre: "sans l'ombre d'un doute, c'est l'esprit . . . le renouveau de Renaissance. . . ."* [20] As a readable work in its genre, it is, nonetheless, greatly overshadowed by illustrious predecessors, primarily as a result of the manner in which Machen handles sensational material. An analysis of his position in this respect is advantageous at this point in his career inasmuch as his greatest period of creativity falls in the 1890's, a decade of more notorious writers.

The Gothic novelists, some of the Romantic poets—Keats, Byron, Shelley—and some of the later Victorians—Swinburne, Rossetti, Symons—utilize, to a great degree, imagery that evokes sensation. While Keats handles the erotic stanzas of "The Eve of St. Agnes" with such delicacy that no feeling stronger than warm tenderness is produced, the Gothic novelists produce horror and terror for the sake of the sensation alone. The feeling of compassion for streetwalkers in De Quincey's *Confessions* and in Dickens' *David Copperfield* is altered to one of admiration in Rossetti's "Jenny," Swinburne's "Dolores," and Symons' "Prostitute," an act which can hardly be construed as anything other than a deliberate affront to Victorian reticence.

Machen's *Chronicle* follows none of the above patterns precisely. Neither does it follow the realistic pattern of the *Decameron* nor the romantic pattern of the heroic cycles. It also lacks the Gargantuan satire of Rabelais, the pretty moral for each tale of *The Heptameron,* and the witty but lecherous tolerance of *Contes Drolatiques.* Machen's tales are almost exclusively about knights and ladies; two deal with seduction and two with cuckoldry; but no direct scenes of a physical nature are portrayed, and indelicate themes are handled purely by the power of suggestion and in a witty manner. By far the most risqué statement in the whole volume is: "It is true that a girl does not object to being tickled, if you do it nicely, and choose the right places. . . ."[21] In short, either because of an inherent fastidiousness or a complete inability to portray character or to provide human motivation, Machen succeeds in conveying no sensation whatsoever.

What, then, is his position toward the use of sensational material? His attitude may best be exemplified by considering one of the typical tales, "How a Knight of Uske Kept Guard over a Tree." Sieur Payne Martell, in attempting to keep a midnight tryst with fair Alianor, is apprehended and besieged in a tree by the father's retainers. Believing their quarry to be safely cornered, they await the dawn to shoot him down; but, to their great bewilderment, they find that he has eluded them. He has discovered the tree to be hollow and has entered into a series of underground passages which end up, oddly enough, in Alianor's chamber. The point of the tale is that we may reach our goal by a crooked path through an opening in an unexpected place.

The deliberate perversion of this and all other morals to the tales can only be interpreted as an intent to shock. His choice of erotic subject matter and his exaltation of the status of ale and drinking are symptoms of his rebellion, just as was the extolling of the virtues of tobacco in *The Anatomy*. Machen desired to kick over the ancestral traces and break away; but, once loose, he did not know quite which direction to take, so he stopped before going too far. He signed his work "Arthur Machen, Silurist" and defined the Silurian position regarding life as the most fantastical comedy. Instead of being coltish, he was rather kittenish. His venture into the field of sensation is so timorous and the result is so innocuous that it was left to his shocking contemporaries, Swinburne and Wilde, to really penetrate the Victorian shell. Machen's work was intellectually conceived and intellectually executed.

In the final analysis, the Romantic nature of the work predominates. It is the spirit of complete withdrawal to the Middle Ages. The sense of the far away and long ago is well executed by the use of courtly material, by such devices as the epistle dedicatory and the pretense of the book's being a translation, and by the masterful handling of archaic diction, with which the seventeenth-century style is often embellished. The reason Brother Drago, Cellarer of the Convent of St. Mary, imbibed too freely "was because he was terribly thirsty, and felt as if a Lollard were being roasted somewhere at the back of his throat. . . ."[22] In another place, a young girl married an old man and pledged her troth "to be bonour and buxom in bed and at board."[23] The subtle constancy to the setting by various means is the most successful element of the tales.

The shortcomings of *The Chronicle* were apprehended almost immediately by the author, and he decided to keep the remaining eight volumes in his head.[24] Thus, like *The Canterbury Tales* and *The Heptameron,* the scope of the work was never fulfilled, apparently because Machen was oppressed by the sense of not having done what he had wanted or what he had visualized in the beginning. Indeed, like Chaucer, Machen later repudiated some of the grosser aspects of the work. When he finished it in an orchard in Gwent in June, 1886, writing atop an old beehive, he composed the requiem, "Here it is, 'The Chronicle of Clemendy': alas!"[25]

The following year was the most eventful one of Machen's life from the point of view of determining his career. He went back to work for Redway at the same salary, at first cataloging books and producing an advertising booklet entitled *Don Quijote de la Mancha.* Then Redway made him editor of *Walford's Antiquarian,* for which he also wrote many unsigned filler articles. His association with this magazine acquainted him with odd bits of information and with old legends and customs which he later incorporated into journalistic essays. This same year he met A. E.

Waite, a devout Catholic and later a reputed scholar of occult movements, who became his lifelong friend. They shared a mutual interest, though a mutual disbelief, in occultism; and Machen solicited articles from Waite for *Walford's*.

On August 31, 1887, Machen married Miss Amelia Hogg, a prominent bachelor girl with independent means, an errant Catholic, thirteen years older than he. Then, on September 29, his father died; and Machen began receiving an inheritance, at first just in trickles, but later on in sufficient amounts to provide him independent means until 1902.

In the interim, with a new wife to support, he changed to the firm of Robson and Karslake, rare book dealers, at an increased salary of £80 a year but still at the onerous task of cataloging and indexing. At the same time, apparently, he and his friend Harry Spurr were trying to break into the rare book and publishing business, because Machen wrote another advertising booklet *Thesaurus Incantatus* for a Thomas Marvell of 98 Great Russell Street, which was his own address. One day, one of his employers asked him to translate a queer duodecimo; and, without knowing or caring what it was, Machen began to turn out what is now the commonly accepted English translation of Casanova's *Memoirs*. In the evenings, for his own amusement, he was engaged in translating Beroalde de Verville's *Le Moyen de Parvenir*, exclusively *sub rosa* literature.

Machen wrote four different translator's notes for the editions of 1894, 1922, 1925, and 1940, which explain quite accurately the history of *The Memoirs* and the difficulty in publication. No other single source recounts with such vividness and historical authenticity the opportunistic atmosphere of the Age of Reason. The problem is that Casanova inserted throughout the many volumes detailed accounts of sexual exploits, both real and imaginary, so that the final product contains large portions of pure pornography. The original manuscript at Leipzig is written in Latin idioms, awkward French, and vulgar and obscene Italian. Machen never saw the original. He worked entirely with the French Sirène Edition, in which the translator Jean Laforgue had clarified some of the obscurities and rounded out the obscenities with witty circumlocutions. Machen's version is complete and strikingly faithful to his text, though many expurgated editions have been issued. In 1893, he invested £1,000 in the publication of the

Memoirs; the printers, Nichols and Smithers, printed and sold a thousand sets for themselves without fear of legal reprisal. The court's opinion would have been that it was just one highwayman robbing another.[26] In 1940, Machen was commissioned to translate the annotations, which had been excluded theretofore.

The other work, de Verville's *Fantastic Tales or the Way to Attain,* as it became in the translation, was so indecent that the printers ran off only four copies of the first seventy-nine pages. They then asked Machen for a revision, which he made by turning all outright offensive passages into clever puns. Later he wrote a preface for the 1923 edition; and in 1929, he was approached by the Hesperides Press to do a more faithful version, but he declined.

By the end of 1889, Machen had served his apprenticeship to the trade. Buoyed up by his marriage, by his inheritance, and by his general worldly success, he decided to strike out on his own, become a free-lance writer, and try to establish his reputation as a creative artist. Thus ended the period of travail which molded his spirit, a period of loneliness, of hunger, of hack work, of immature writing, with *The Chronicle of Clemendy* as an end of it all. After his Aunt Maria's death in 1891, his last link with Caerleon, the fort of the legion, was broken. It was his home no more, but it was never out of his mind. London was henceforth his destiny, and the next ten years were to prove the most fruitful of his entire existence.

II *Sion and Bagdad*

By 1890, Machen's legacy provided him with an income of £400 to £500 annually for several years.[27] Although he began a course of semi-lavish living, contracted for a cottage in the Chiltern Hills, took a trip to France every year until 1898, and lived mainly on his capital instead of investing his money, Machen realized, nonetheless, that this was his one chance to succeed. He wrote voluminously—essays, short stories, odds and ends and varieties for papers, turnovers for *The Globe,* articles for the *St. James's Gazette,* the first part of "The Great God Pan" for *The Whirlwind,* as well as "smart" tales, like "Resurrectio Mortuorum," for an almost extinct family of journals or "society" papers, such as the *World.*

Socially and intellectually, Machen was never in the center of the milieu of the 1890's, but he touched the outer periphery at many points. Without doubt, the nature of his acquaintance with Oscar Wilde best illustrates Machen's position. Wilde's *The Picture of Dorian Gray* had just been published; and Machen, inferring from a passage in it that Wilde might enjoy *Fantastic Tales,* sent him a copy. As a result of this gesture, Machen received an invitation to dine at the Florence, an Italian restaurant in Rupert Street. Wilde praised Machen's "The Double Return," in the *St. James's Gazette,* as the story that "fluttered the dovecotes." Machen found Wilde to be a brilliant, extremely witty entertainer and without affectation in the ordinary sense, but entirely superficial in all topics of conversation. They dined together at the same place once more that year, but never became intimate friends. In 1892, Machen accidentally met Wilde again, and this time Wilde was furious that his *Salome* had not been licensed. They met for the last time in 1895 in a publisher's office after Wilde's character had been publicly denounced. Machen found him to be a shocking sight, "a great mass of rosy fat . . . like an obese old Frenchwoman in man's clothes," and completely horrifying.[28]

With the exception of seeing a few plays, such as Ibsen's *Ghosts* or a Henry Irving production, Machen spent most of the period writing. From 1891 to 1893, at his cottage in Buckinghamshire, he finished *The Great God Pan and the Inmost Light* and two other tales which embraced the concept of *The Three Impostors.* Of the latter work, he saved only "The Novel of the Dark Valley" and destroyed the rest. Not happy with the Chiltern Hills, he moved back to 36 Great Russell Street. The publication of *The Great God Pan and the Inmost Light* by John Lane, the famous publisher of Bodley Head, with illustrations by the *Yellow Book* artist Aubrey Beardsley, created considerable sensation. Parodies were written; and when Mr. Mudie sold a copy of the book, he always brought it from under the counter. Lane also published *The Three Impostors,* but its appearance was coincident with the scandals of 1895. It had, therefore, an unfavorable reception as a distinctly unhealthy book.[29]

Despite Machen's intentions in 1889 to abandon his ancient mode of writing,[30] he had still not developed a modern style of his own. After reading much adverse critical comment ranking him as a second-rate imitator of Stevenson,[31] Machen resolved to dispense with the black and white magic and to amend his style so that it could not be mistaken for that of someone else.[32]

From his new quarters at 4 Verulam Buildings, Gray's Inn, where he lived until 1901, he wandered aimlessly through the London streets in the company of his bulldog Juggernaut; the same sense of isolation came upon him that he had felt during his first sojourn at Clarendon Road. At this time, in October, 1895, he conceived the idea for *The Garden of Avallaunius,* afterwards called *The Hill of Dreams,* as a *Robinson Crusoe* of the soul.[33]

In February, 1896, he set down the first word and continued to write steadily for slightly over a year. He found the task difficult because this book was the only one which he tried to write according to a prearranged plan and in a style completely his own. Consequently, he was confronted with constant revision and with the rewriting of several chapters. In March, 1897, this unique novel was completed; but Machen could find no publisher for it at the time. He also put together a queer assortment of tales, mood impressions, and prose poems under the title *Ornaments in Jade.* That book, too, found its way into a desk drawer.[34]

At a tavern gathering in Gray's Inn in 1897, Machen and George Moore were arguing the merits of Celtic literature; and as a result of the attention Machen directed toward himself, the host of the evening pressed him into the service of *Literature,* forerunner of *The Times Literary Supplement,*[35] the first issue of which appeared on October 23. For about one year Machen wrote book reviews and some leading articles. After he quit the magazine he renewed his creative efforts with concentrated energy and finished "The White People" in April, 1899; *Hieroglyphics* in May; and the first part of *A Fragment of Life* in June. Each of these was written in a different style.

His current literary endeavors and almost his whole literary career were brought to a halt by the death of his wife on July 31, 1899, "*apres douze ans d'un mariage très uni. . . .*"[36] Machen loved his wife very deeply, and her slow and painful death from cancer left so deep a wound that he never mentioned her name thereafter. Whenever he refers to the episode at all in his works, it is always neatly cloaked in symbol. After six years of lamentable expectation, he felt that his life had been dashed into fragments:[37] "Then a great sorrow which had long threatened fell upon me: I was once more alone."[38] By some mysterious process, like self-hypnotism induced perhaps by prayer, his prostrating grief was changed to an almost intolerable ecstasy, a profound emotional change from great torment to deep peace.[39] Though the impulse to write was gone, he at any rate recovered his equanimity sufficiently to throw himself into the social milieu by the end of the year. He met Edgar Jepson and Max Beerbohm at this time and, in November, entertained for about a week P. J. Toulet, the French translator of *The Great God Pan.*

In reviewing the climactic period of Machen's life, 1890 to 1900, the evidence is clear that he achieved neither riches nor fame. Only two of his books were published, both tales of the weird and occult; some of his better tales appeared only in the transient medium of periodicals; and some of his other masterworks were not even published at all. As a consequence, his position in the world of letters by 1900, despite his great productivity and his almost frantic attempts to establish a reputation, differed only in slight degree from what it was at the time he had first set pen to paper. However, from this defeat, he emerged the victor in many ways. Spiritually he had withstood life's greatest sorrow, and intellectually he had matured to the point where he could cast off the mannerisms and philosophies of other writers and declare himself to the world. He openly embraced the cause of the idealists, the anti-materialists, the romanticists, and the mystics. Though he was bruised and lacked for the first time the courage to write, instead of permanent frustration and embitterment, a state of militant retirement set in, the readiness to speak out for the truth as he saw it whenever the opportunity availed itself.

This brief perspective study of Machen's life has thus far established one fact quite clearly: though Machen wrote a great portion of his work in the 1890's, the period itself denied him. Therefore, the problem, which will be analyzed in later chapters, is to critically evaluate works primarily written in and for one age but not recognized or appreciated until another.

III *Bensonian Memories*

The year 1900 was one of reorientation and adjustment for this lonely, bearded man as he desperately sought society and did strange things in an effort to find a new pattern of life—even to the extent of joining the Rosicrucian Order of the Golden

Dawn of which Waite, W. B. Yeats, and Aleister Crowley were members. Finally, however, through Christopher Wilson, Machen established his course of life for the next nine years by joining the Benson Shakespeare Repertory Company. He was partially concerned with earning a living, but he was even more concerned with getting out of himself.

His prior knowledge of the theatre was extremely limited, so for a novice his professional associations could not have been more fortunate. The Benson Company was blessed in that the members of the troupe took joy in their work, teaching beginners the right and wrong way to stand and other fundamentals of acting.[40] The Benson method did the utmost to produce proficient actors, and the group formed a kind of fellowship, a mystery in the craft sense: "The memories come, the memories pass, the music dies down, and Lear's hunting horn sounds no more. The Old Bensonians part, and some of those whom fate has forced into paths that are different indeed, wonder how it was once possible to live by an art and craft followed with joy and delight and pleasure, even to its smallest detail. But such a fellowship, such a company, such a mystery, may a Man make, even in these days."[41]

In order to maintain a continuous sustenance, Machen left his stand-on, walk-on, one-line parts with Benson to play small but varied roles at the Gaiety, the St. James' Theatre, and on tour with Sir Beerbohm Tree, George Alexander, Garnet Holme, and others. This life brought him into contact with many famous actors, actresses, managers, and playwrights—Walter Hampden, Ellen Terry, Leon Quartermaine, and Stephen Phillips. Later in life, when Machen was revealing to the public the mental processes behind his literary creations, he casually mentioned that Henry Irving once told him, "Never take people behind the scenes."[42] But despite the proximity of such illustrious personages, the art of theatrics never brushed off on Machen to any great degree. He was at heart always a man of letters.

After the publication of *Hieroglyphics* in 1902 and his marriage to Dorothie Purefoy Hudleston on June 25, 1903, he gradually drifted back to writing between theatrical engagements. He took up exactly where he had left off years before by finishing *A Fragment of Life.* Waite, who formerly had used some of Machen's work in *The Unknown World,* was now editor of *Hor-*

lick's Magazine and provided some encouragement, not only by publishing his new work, but also "The White People" and *The Garden of Avallaunius.*

A Fragment of Life, which developed from one of his early short stories "Resurrectio Mortuorum," is written in two different styles: it begins with naturalism and ends with intonation. It marks a shift in approach and subject matter from the black magic and demonology of the 1890's to the more positive revelation of miracles and communion which he was to adopt thereafter. It purports to express the inexpressible, to rend the veil through the regaining of ancestral consciousness, which, to Machen, meant realigning oneself with the Celtic spirit. The genesis of the story arose from his seeing a father, mother, and child—all in colorless attire and with vacuous expressions—get on a tram in London: "And yet, I said to myself, these two have partaken together of the great mystery, of the great sacrament of nature, of the source of all that is magical in the wide world. But have they discerned the mysteries? Do they know that they have been in that place which is called Syon and Jerusalem?" [43]

The interior tale is concerned with the life of a common clerk, who is separated from his wife by practicalities and Victorian reticence. His one desire is to break through the barriers that separate them, and the moment of realization of that dream comes when he begins to live an inner life through the discovery of old Welsh documents in the attic. The final ecstatic communion is realized when he and his wife go to live in a Welsh mansion which he inherits. Machen, here, is simply using daily routine as a foil to heighten the intensity of the passion and sudden rapture that can turn the dull flesh of man to fire.[44] "Darnell knew by experience that man is made a mystery for mysteries and visions, for the realization in his consciousness of ineffable bliss, for a great joy that transmutes the whole world, for a joy that surpasses all joys and overcomes all sorrows." [45]

To bridge the gap between the real world and that of mystic idealism, Machen describes a church wherein are performed mystic ceremonies and elaborate and curious rites embodied in a mystery language, until it becomes a symbol of the whole world, of a "great ceremony or sacrament, which teaches under visible forms a hidden and transcendent doctrine." [46] Also used to penetrate the veil and to pass into the supernal regions beyond are phrases and symbols appearing in earlier works, such as the mystic fragrance of incense. On the other hand, hints of black magic and a girl's shriek are symbols of the dangers and pitfalls that lie in wait for one who clings to material life and fears to cast off on an uncharted course. For Darnell, returning to Wales represents a renunciation of worldly life; but, in return, he discovers love and the vision of the Graal.

A Fragment of Life is an attempt to penetrate the seeming void in the lives of mediocre and limited people, who live in such places as Long Street where the houses are all alike, by assuming that they also have partaken of everlasting mysteries and of great secrets "and have known what is concealed under the barley in the sacred basket of the holy procession of Eleusis."[47] Sound though the premise may be, that all individuals have their ethereal moments, the task of penetrating the sacrosanct and inviolable realm of the human spirit is an unsurmountable one; for that which is inarticulate cannot be voiced and that which is without image cannot be reflected. This work is Machen's nearest approach to expressing the inexpressible, but it is so nebulous and remote from common experience that it has had only a small body of readers in the past—and even that number is steadily diminishing.

In 1906, Grant Richards published Machen's *The House of Souls,* which, except for *A Fragment of Life,* contained works that had been completed prior to 1900. In the preface Machen satirized puritanical intolerance of all art devoid of a moral purpose. He suggested an elaboration of the preface to a publisher and, as a result, received a contract to write a book which he entitled *Dr. Stiggins: His Views and Principles*. This book, which St. John Adcock referred to as Machen's one failure,[48] is totally a satire upon Protestantism with incidental forays upon Puritanism and America.

Dr. Stiggins, a Free Churchman, defends Cromwell, Milton, divorce, American democracy, and men of business; belittles history and our corrupt theatre; and deplores immoral art of all sorts. Machen is denouncing Dr. Stiggins through his own banal, commercial, and ridiculous views. The tone of harangue and uncurbed intolerance is quite out of harmony with Machen's other works and did nothing to enhance his reputation as a creative writer. In fact, *Dr. Stiggins* was hardly noticed at the time and has received even less attention since.

On May 17, 1906, Machen was introduced to the members of the New Bohemians Club, of which he later became secretary, a club devoted to the debate of controversial topics, mainly literary and artistic. On one occasion Lord Alfred Douglas, editor of *The Academy,* was invited as a guest; and soon after his visit, many members, Machen included, were asked to write for his magazine. Machen's position corresponded to that of religious editor. He reviewed most of the books on religion, but he also submitted articles on varied subjects which, taken together, are the most lucid and straightforward account of his beliefs ever published. They will be considered in a later chapter.

In 1907, Richards published *The Hill of Dreams,* which attracted some critical acclaim, although it never became anything close to a best seller. In the same year, Machen, despite his journalistic commitments and another stage role, found time to start *The Secret Glory,* which he finished in 1908. It was not published until fourteen years later.

Five years before, Machen had played the role of an Argive elder in the chorus of an Orestean trilogy—*The Agammemnon, The Libation Bearers,* and *The Furies*—which the Benson Company had taken on a public-school tour. The students at Harrow insulted, hounded, and brutally treated the band of strolling players, an incident which Machen never forgot and which led him to satirize the English public-school system in *The Secret Glory*. The book, half satire and half mysticism, is imperfectly blended. Machen's explanation for the almost totally unrelated aspects was that he had been reading the lives of famous schoolmasters and, the next year, had been investigating the legend of the Holy Graal. Like the critic of the *Eatanswill Gazette* who reviewed a work on Chinese metaphysics by reading metaphysics under "M" and China under "C" in the *Encyclopaedia Britannica,* Machen combined his information.[49]

Though Machen's facetious explanation in no way blends the disparate elements into a unified work of art, his purpose is nonetheless lucidly apparent. He is countering the antithesis with the thesis: he opposes materialism and spirituality to denigrate the former. In *A Fragment of Life,* he sets a mundane, meaningless, and commonplace existence against the ecstasy of mystical discovery. In *Dr. Stiggins* he accomplishes the same end by means of irony: the Doctor castigates himself through his crass and material views. In *The Secret Glory* Ambrose Meyrick, a sensitive student at Lupton, is bullied and beaten by the other boys and by the master Mr. Horbury, his uncle, until he finds hidden strength in his contempt for their narrow standards; whips his fellow students; becomes a star athlete; a model student; and, with expectations great for him, runs off to London with Nelly Foran, a chambermaid; writes an obscene, Rabelaisian epistle to Horbury; becomes a strolling player; goes to Kevir and is crucified by the Turks. The ending is obviously foreign to the work and may simply have been a way for Machen to vent his malice at the students of Harrow for their barbaric treatment of the Benson Company. As far as the satire is concerned, Machen makes the point of it explicitly clear; the real values of life are hidden from the casual gaze; the modern world is worshiping a monster; there are a hundred doors to the garden of delight but we open one to a cesspool.[50]

The positive side of Machen's thesis is revealed through the notebooks of Meyrick, which not only are romantic devices to establish remoteness and removal from common life, but also are symbols of the secret and spiritual life within. The story of Ambrose is intended as a direct parallel of the Graal legend, and in it the spiritual unpreparedness of the recipients of the symbol of their faith causes its withdrawal. Pervading the legend is the deep sense of loss and the penance of constant search and renunciation of worldly things. In Ambrose's case the "attainment of the mystic sanctity—the achieving of the Graal" [51]—comes through the renunciation of physical love, which Machen summarized axiomatically: " 'If you desire love: refrain from the Beloved.' " [52]

Although the illicit liaison with Nelly Foran comes close to the *fin de siècle* spirit of shocking the moral sensibilities of an outmoded generation, Machen uses her rather as a symbol of a love to be renounced. The young man and woman pass their days in constant discovery of the rarities and wonders of the world until their unutterable joy began to be unbearable. Ambrose then reveals in his notebook that he is on the verge of breaking off their intimacy because he feels that its prolongation would consume him utterly: "'I should pass away in delight because our bodies are not meant to live for long in the middle of white fire.'" [53]

When Nelly tells him of employers who attempted to seduce her, Ambrose begins to sense his own sin: "'All heedless, without knowledge, without preparation, without receiving the mystic word, I had stumbled into the shrine, uninitiated I had passed beyond the veil and gazed upon the hidden mystery, on the secret glory that is concealed from the holy angels.'" [54] With that realization comes the ultimate determination to renounce her: "'I had never known all her strange allurement before. I had refined and symbolized and made her into a sign of joy, and now before me she shone disarrayed—not a symbol, but a woman, in the new intelligence that had come to me, and I longed for her. I had just enough strength and no more.'" [55]

Machen's imagery in the mystical portion of the book is exclusively from Wales: place names, description, and references to the rite of the Cor-arbennic and to famous mythical personages from *The Mabinogion.* Closely connected to the lives of the Welsh saints is the allusion to a fictitious ancient chapel, appearing more than once in Machen's works, which is symbolic of his theory that the Celtic church is associated with the Great Errantry, with the search for Avalon. As far as Machen was concerned, Anglicanism was good; but Celtic sanctity and the ancient mass of the Britons was better.[56] Meyrick is graced with the opportunity of seeing a splendid chalice, the Holy Cup of Teilo Sant, which in the beauty of its creation seems undoubtedly to be the work of God; but an admonition is issued to those who view the ancient rites unprepared: "*Woe and great sorrow are on him, for he hath looked unworthily into the Tremendous Mysteries, and on the Secret Glory which is hidden from the Holy Angels.*" [57] Ambrose bears witness "for the old faith, for the faith of secret and beautiful and hidden mysteries. . . ." [58]

Unfortunately, the symbolism was too esoteric for any publisher to take a chance; or, as Machen put it in the words of Ambrose, in prose works often "'the symbolism is inadequate; but that is the defect of speech of any kind when you have once ventured beyond the multiplication table and the jargon of the Stock Exchange. Inadequacy of expression is merely a minor part of the great tragedy of humanity.'" [59] Machen put aside his unwanted manuscript and continued to write for *The Academy* until August, 1908, when T. W. H. Crosland's new editorial policy of no payment to contributors forced him to switch to *T. P.'s Weekly,* for which he wrote until 1910. One of Machen's last articles in *The Academy* was a tribute to Benson, an exposé of the insecure tenure and meager salaries of actors, and his farewell to the Benson Company.[60] Actually he did not quit the stage, however, until the spring of 1909, when he played the part of Bolingbroke, the enchanter, in *Henry VI, Part II.* In a letter to D. P. M. Michael, Machen wrote: "So far as I know, I am the only actor who ever wrote his part in Shakespeare. It was exactly the farewell to the stage that I should have chosen. . . ." [61]

Acting had served its purpose, provided him with a living, and forced him out of mourning. His Thespian instincts, however, had never been deep-rooted. Married again and with all of his work of the 1890's published or republished—notwithstanding the small treatment that it received at the hands of the public—his dogged, persevering streak pulled him once more toward his former career and demanded that the writer earn his bread by writing.

IV *The Ugly Toad*

This rationale led him into a period of existence which he termed "prostitution of the soul." [62] In 1910, he became a journalist for *The Evening News.* At first, the reality may not have seemed so abhorrent and compromising because it was the profession for which his parents long ago had wished him to prepare and for which he had studied shorthand for many years. His position was the rather exalted one of chief reporter to cover state ceremonies and great occasions, and it seemed only a step at the time from selling articles to magazines. Thus, in his advancing years, he settled down to servitude and became a family man, had a son, Arthur Blaize Hilary, in 1912 and a daughter, Janet, in 1917, the support of whom was made possible through his job "to lick spittle from the office floor." [63]

The experience was a humbling one, because for the first time in many years he had to work at the direction of an outside force rather than in conformance with certain subjective standards. He worked from 10 A.M. to about 3 A.M.; and if no stories worthy of his mettle were in the making, he was given an ordinary assignment. Thus, although he wrote on the coronation ceremony of

George V, on Winston Churchill as Home Secretary, and on the father of Anthony Eden, he also interviewed Stephen Phillips and Sir Arthur Quiller-Couch and covered championship billiard matches and poltergeist cases. He also wrote some reviews, among which was a highly laudatory appraisal of John Masefield's *Everlasting Mercy*.

In 1914, destiny, backhanded and perverse as it often is, converted Machen's greatest trial into his one moment of glory. As he said, "the newspaper business, though, like the toad, ugly and venomous, has yet its precious jewels scattered here and there on its squalid vestments." [64] In August he read an account of the retreat from Mons in the *Weekly Dispatch;* and in a supernatural war story, appearing on September 29, he convinced a multitude of people for once that what he had written was true.[65]

"The Bowmen" had been to him at the time of conception a disappointing story; but it became his one popular success, though the newspaper received the remuneration. It opened the door to the only fame ever to come his way during his lifetime. Turner, the editor, cognizant of the commercial possibilities of the subject, engaged Machen to write several other stories of a similar nature—"Soldiers' Rest," "The Monstrance," and "The Dazzling Light." All of these stories were collected and published under the title of *The Angels of Mons.*

On the strength of his success, Machen was permitted to write four long works for *The Evening News: The Great Return,* released serially in 1915; *The Confessions of a Literary Man,* the autobiographical work known better by the later title of *Far Off Things; The Great Terror,* later just *The Terror,* 1916; and *God and the War,* later entitled *War and the Christian Faith,* 1917. In 1918 he wrote another supernatural story, "Drake's Drum," further exploiting the style and idea of "The Bowmen." Both *The Terror* and "Drake's Drum" were widely circulated in England and the United States in various periodicals.

In *The Great Return,* Machen adopted the guise of a reporter investigating the strange doings and remarkable occurrences at Llantrisant. The church was exquisite with the odor of rare gums, although the rector said he used no incense. The service was a queer one, though not of the dissenting tribes; and a bright light was seen emanating from some inexplicable source. Miracles began to occur, feuds were reconciled, and the reporter saw a look of ineffable joy on a stranger's face. A child and a deaf woman heard a bell, like a bell ringing in Paradise, the wonderful bell of Teilo Sant. Sailors saw a red spark on Chapel Head, the Rose of Fire, and all aches and pains left them. Olwen Phillips, a tubercular, dreamed of a bell, of three men in blood-colored robes with a blue, jeweled altar, and of a cup like a rose with blood in it; and she awoke well. She had had a vision of the Holy Graal. All churchgoers attended Llantrisant, and the folk memory returned in the ancient ceremony of the Mass of the Sangraal.

All of Machen's mystical devices are included in *The Great Return* and greatly elaborated—the incense, the bells, the church, the rose, the holy cup of Teilo Sant, and the vision of the Graal. As far as the materials are concerned, nothing new has been added, except that the approach has assumed a ritualistic tone almost in the manner of one experienced in seduction—the wine, the flowers, the low music, the dim lights, and then the grand passion. The mechanical features of the book are exaggerated, rather than diminished, by the reportorial style, which is not particularly adaptable to the uses of the mystic. Broadly speaking, the work is not one of Machen's best efforts; and its greatest significance is that it shows his ever-increasing trend toward religiosity.

War and the Christian Faith is an expository work, essentially his articles of religious belief. He maintains that faith is an adventure and that man is born to sail through unknown seas.[66] But his experience gives the search new meaning: "So when the great voyage draws to an end, we may be amazed to find that the new haven is in fact the old, though it has been wonderfully transmuted. . . . And the roses; they sway over the hedgerows as of old; but they are the roses of paradise." [67] He reiterates his doctrine of the mysteries: "The truth is that, whether we like it or not, we live, if we live well, in and by and through mysteries." [68] To further confound the Protestants and some of the wayward Anglo-Catholic clergy, he asserts that faith, not morals, is the supreme end of life. It is the key to all mysteries, the fulfillment of all desires, the quest of all quests. Galahad sought more than respectability, journeyed on a stranger adventure, sought a nobler chalice than the cup in which non-alcoholic beverages are contained.[69]

The Confessions of a Literary Man is a strongly romanticized account of the major influences in Machen's life to 1886. Charmingly written, it is a series of discursive personal essays that unfortunately reveal few facts of his life. What Machen mainly emphasizes is the importance of his Welsh background, a subject that will be discussed later in connection with the analysis of his key works.

"Drake's Drum," another supernatural dream-vision tale on the order of "The Bowmen," exploits a wartime theme. As the English fleet prepares to take possession of the German fleet, a roll of drums is heard and the spirit of Drake intervenes in the tense atmosphere to prevent further hostilities. It is clearly a sequel, prompted by the success of his earlier tale, and has no great merit of its own.

The Terror, the other work published in *The Evening News,* is a unique mystery story and will be analyzed later; but at the time of publication it served to attract attention to earlier volumes, which had almost faded into oblivion, and to promote a revival of interest in Machen as an author. In this decade he had met certain fairly eminent personages by virtue of his slight fame as an author, rather than in his capacity as a reporter. As a guest of the Square Club, he had met John Galsworthy and other notables, but Machen found the atmosphere too stuffy and declined to join. Later he met Holbrook Jackson and Gilbert Seldes. None of these authors or scholars, however, felt keenly enough about his talents to make special efforts on his behalf.

In 1917 Machen's star began to rise. At the age of fifty-four, he made *Who's Who;* and in America, Vincent Starrett, who had read *The Terror* and then searched out *The House of Souls* and *The Hill of Dreams,* proclaimed his genius and stated unequivocally that Machen ranked with Cervantes, Rabelais, and Boccaccio.[70] The following year Starrett struck up a correspondence with Machen and was given full license to take whatever he liked from *The Academy* and *T. P.'s Weekly.*[71] Likewise, Ben Hecht, who visited Machen on a trip to London, gave him some publicity in Chicago newspapers, though Hecht and Machen were not in accord as to the nature of true literature.

Machen changed over to *The Daily Express* for a brief period in 1918, but he returned to his old job the following year. By this time he began to have a glimmering of hope when Alfred A. Knopf, to whom Machen was recommended by Carl Van Vechten,[72] asked for some manuscript for his Borzoi books. On the strength of these expectations, Machen moved to better quarters at St. John's Wood, where he lived until 1927. James Branch Cabell, although not a personal friend, was, at least, a kindred spirit who helped promote Machen's cause: "But here in a secluded library is no place to speak of the thirty years' neglect that has been accorded Mr. Arthur Machen: it is the sort of crime that ought to be discussed in the Biblical manner, from the housetop. . . ." [73] The following year, 1920, brought another American champion to his doorstep, Paul Jordan-Smith, who denounced the world for making "one of the greatest artists of our time . . . a journalist and 'a past master in the Lodge of Disappointment.'" [74]

With such unexpected eloquence on his side and with the republication of his works relatively assured on both sides of the Atlantic, Machen, at the age of fifty-eight, broke with his life of worse than penal servitude. Although ostensibly sacked because of a legal suit over a false obituary he had written about Lord Alfred Douglas,[75] Machen was relieved to sever his association with *The Evening News* and left with these parting words: "*Eduxit me de lacu miseriae, et de luto faecis. Et statuit super petram pedes meos: et direxit gressus meos.*" [76]

Despite his contempt for journalism, the degrading profession had provided him with the twofold opportunity for enriching his experience and for promoting his fame. In addition, it served him by altering his nature from frenzied irritation to mellow calm. Whereas in 1906 he could scarcely conceal his malaise and intolerance of things as they were, in 1921 he found it difficult to display malice toward the institutions he most detested. By an alchemical or magical transformation, the years became golden and replete with wisdom. From satire he turned to the personal essay; from worldly things, to eternity; for, when he had learned no longer to hope, the dream of his youth was fulfilled.

V Dog and Duck

The revival of interest in Machen's works in the 1920's among publishers, readers, and collectors was somewhat of an anomaly. In one sense the republication of nearly all of his works by Martin Secker in London and by Knopf in New York constituted a discovery rather than a rediscovery because few of his works had been published in the 1890's and the sporadic and restricted editions that followed had not caught on. From eighteen titles, including the translations, in print between the years 1881 and 1922, he received only £635.[77]

On the surface, the literary temper of the two periods does not correspond. The belated Romance of the last decade of the nineteenth century does not equate with the Realism of Mencken, Hecht, Fitzgerald, or Hemingway. Although in historical perspective the Realistic school emerged predominant, the 1920's was, nonetheless, a decade of wild unrest, of crazy fads, of experimentation, and of search for new values. In this respect, a definite parallel exists between the earlier Aesthetic-Decadent school, with which Machen was tangentially connected, and such writers of the 1920's as Van Vechten and Cabell. Critical analogies, however, are not completely satisfying. When writers like John Dos Passos and Robert Hillyer, orbits apart in thinking and literary techniques, could both be impressed by Machen at the same time, the assumption must be made that his works have some intrinsic merit.

At any rate, though the sales of each volume were small, collectively thousands of copies of his various works came off the presses, enough to insure his survival, at least in a small way, for several generations, even had his books never been reprinted. Secker continued publication until 1926; Knopf, until 1928. Unfortunately, the period of renown came too belatedly for Machen to exploit it on any grand scale. He had no bureau full of manuscript and his creative urge was in its Indian summer. In February, 1922, *The Secret Glory* was salvaged from the rejected file and met the public for the first time, as did *Ornaments in Jade* in 1924. Also, he carefully screened the periodicals to which he had contributed in the past for worthy material. Besides all of the creative works in *The Evening News,* which were either published for the first time in book form or republished, several volumes were gleaned from similar sources: *Strange Roads,* Starrett's *The Shining Pyramid* and *The Glorious Mystery,* Secker's *The Shining Pyramid, Dog and Duck, Notes and Queries,* and *Dreads and Drolls.* With the exception of the last, most of the selections are expository or personal essays, which will be discussed later.

The essays and tales in *Dreads and Drolls* were composed, as the author admitted, from veridical and imaginative sources. He selected material which in its bare facts read "like a subtle study in mysterious suggestion, a ghost story of the rarest kind." [78] The stories which he thought worthy of retelling and the original ones which he composed on the same pattern all have in common a note of mysteriousness which he felt that only the talent of the true artist could project: "This is a great gift: to be able so to tell the bare truth that it seems a magnificent lie. To many of us it is rather given to invent elaborate fictions which are plainer (and duller) than the plainest facts." [79]

In the dread category, "The Man with the Silver Staff" is a story of the famous clown Joe Grimaldi, whose life was edited by Dickens. Grimaldi was invited to the home of a supposedly wealthy gentleman, Mr. Mackintosh; when he arrived, he found it was merely a roadside tavern. Later he was invited to the real Mackintosh mansion in London where he enjoyed the Arabian hospitality of twelve desperate characters who simply wanted to be amused. The second story, also of Joe Grimaldi, "The Adventure of the Long-Lost Brother," is concerned with the appearance of Joe's wandering brother at the dressing room of the theatre where Grimaldi was appearing. While Joe dressed for the street, the brother disappeared, and Joe never saw him again, though each person whom Joe interrogated had seen the brother only moments before.

Most of the stories are from famous newspaper mysteries or from books of the eighteenth century. "The Campden Wonder" is such a one. It was also the basis of a play by Masefield, produced in 1907 by H. Granville Barker. In this tale a servant confesses to the murder of his employer, Mr. Harrison; three people are executed on the basis of the confession without any *corpus delicti*. After some years Mr. Harrison returns, having been abducted and taken on a Turkish ship to Smyrna. Other murders and disappearances probably taken from journalistic sources are "The Euston Square Mystery," "The Highbury Mystery," and "The Strange Case of Emily Weston." From the *Annual Register* and old law annals, he derived the substance of such recapitulations as "Mr. Lutterloh" and "The Ingenious Mr. Blee." Machen utilized the occult notion of the existence of alter egos or exact doubles in " 'Doubles' in Crime." In the recount of the Highbury mystery, Machen presents the occultists' claim that the astral body of the murderer stayed in the counting house and that the murder was committed by the spirit body.

In the droll category, Machen utilized his more general knowledge of the eighteenth century to create many of the essays and tales. In this group are "Morduck the Witch," "How Clubs Began," "Before Wembley," "A Lament for London's Lost Inns," "More Inns," "Deadly Nevergreen," and "Ceremony on the Scaffold." Emanating from Machen's zest for Boswell's *Life of Johnson* are "Polite Correspondence" and "Old Dr. Mounsey." Reflecting a specialized interest in eighteenth century affairs as the translator of Casanova's *Memoirs* is "Casanova in London."

Machen deals with two of his favorite topics in "The Little People" and "Chivalry." In "How the Rich Live," he makes casual use of the little-exploited phase of his career as an actor. "7B Coney Court" is a tale, obviously fabricated, of a nonexistent tenant in the upstairs lumber room who pays his rent regularly and requests in writing that repairs be made on his lodgings. The very nature of the works clearly indicates a certain disposition on Machen's part to commercialize upon his brief period of popularity. The fact that he had to rely almost wholly upon source material for his inspiration is a clear manifestation that his creative powers were on the wane.

In fact, Machen did nothing completely new or original during the whole decade with the exception of *Dog and Duck*. He had to rely greatly on reminiscences and previously acquired knowledge to fulfill the demands of the publishers: *Things Near and Far,* a continuation of his autobiographical *Far Off Things,* written in the same style and covering the period 1886 to 1921; *The London Adventure,* a smattering of events that took place during his journalistic career; Henry Danielson's *Arthur Machen, A Bibliography,* for which Machen wrote notes on the origins of his works written before 1923; *Fleet Street Diversions and Digressions,* more reminiscences from his newspaper days, which the publisher never released; an introduction to a new edition of Casanova's *Memoirs;* introductions for the Knopf editions; and numerous introductions for the works of others, in which he reiterated mostly what he had already written before.

Under pressure to produce something new, he completed *The Canning Wonder,* a repetitive documentary of an eighteenth-century trial; but even in this documentary account the mystery remains as profound and insoluble as in the original source material. His consideration of it lends only a vague hint of the occult to Elizabeth Canning's inexplicable disappearance for thirty days. As in his explanation for the general appearance of visionary creatures who aided the English soldiers in the war, he offers the possible solution of collective hallucination or delusion; but in order to introduce a hint of the supernatural he makes note of the "cunning man": an astrologer, whom Elizabeth's mother consulted in an attempt to arrive at the truth of the matter.

To try to keep up with the demand, Machen really struck the bottom of the barrel when he released *Precious Balms,* thirty years of reviews about his own works, and when he wrote outright advertisements for book sellers. By 1925 his popularity among first-edition book collectors had fallen to a low, and he had almost no writing to do. After 1926 the Knopf editions were a glut on the second-hand market. If Charles Parsons, an American collector, who later presented Yale with his Machen collection, had not purchased the only extant copy of *Eleusinia* from Machen for £100, young Hilary Machen might have been precipitously withdrawn from Merchant Taylors' School at the beginning of the second term. By 1927 the half yearly royalties from Knopf amounted to twenty-five dollars;[80] his poverty was apparently great when he appeared at Claridge's in 1928 in his eccentric cape, a threadbare suit, and a hat too small for his head, to contract with Bennett Cerf for an introduction to Smollett's *Humphry Clinker* in the Modern Library edition. His spirit, however, was unimpaired as he downed a decanter of wine and polished off his contemporaries one by one. He seemed eager to accept $100 and brought in the introduction the next morning.[81]

Though the end of the decade found Machen in worse circumstances than those from which he had been rescued, he still had seen a moment of glory, with book collectors putting a high value on Machen rarities. Parsons had paid $1,000 for the manuscript of *The Hill of Dreams;* and the first edition of *Fantastic Tales* brought $210 at the Quinn sale in 1924. As a minor celebrity and genial host, Machen was much sought after, particularly by visiting Americans. Among his visitors were Elinor Wylie, Alfred Goldsmith, Robert Hillyer, Hunter Stagg, Montgomery Evans, III, Parsons, Starrett, Jordan-Smith, and Knopf. He was even interviewed in 1925 by a promising young journalist named John Gunther, who saw Machen as a twentieth-century Johnson with the same witty, deep-toned, Latinized dialogue; odd yet striking in appearance, with red glazed cheeks which jelled when he laughed; thick white hair done in a horizontal bob; clouded blue eyes; and waxen hands.[82] In fact, Machen once played the role of Dr. Johnson in a film never released. His guests came, however, not only to savor the witty repartee, but also to sip his famous Dog and Duck punch.

His semilavish living came to a halt. Publications ceased, and book collectors eased off. Machen was compelled once more to work for hire in order to eke out a subsistence, this time with the publishing firm of Benn, who paid him £250 per year as a reader for prospective publications. As a supplement to this meager income, his friend Hillyer in America invented an unknown benefactress and sent him a few thousand dollars from 1928 through 1930. Also, Evans brought gifts frequently and sent food parcels when away. With such assistance Machen was able to move to Old Amersham, Buckinghamshire, where he spent the rest of his days. During 1929 he had only two requests for his writing: one, to put the grossness back in Beroalde de Verville, a commission which he turned over to a young friend Oliver Stonor; another, to produce a new work for an American publisher. The result was *Tom O'Bedlam,* an expository essay, reiterating in a slightly different way Machen's fundamental beliefs. He had long since said all that he had to say many times.

VI *The Civil List*

Machen's declining years were not spent in poverty, thanks to the many staunch friends he had made. When Hillyer was forced by the depression to discontinue his assistance, Evans, John Gawsworth, Jepson, and others petitioned for a civil-list pension on Machen's behalf. Starting in 1933 he received £100 per year. Although Benn cut off his salary in the same year, he continued to write for Benn's magazine and received commissions from time to time from other periodicals to do book reviews and articles. Beginning in 1936, Oliver Stonor made Machen a small donation yearly for seven years. On his seventy-fourth birthday he received recognition from Wales in the form of a £200 check presented with due ceremony. In 1938 his pension was increased to £140, though the rising cost of living no doubt destroyed any tangible benefits. Thus, when some of his English acquaintances looked him up during World War II, he was living in straitened circumstances; and a committee consisting of George Bernard

Shaw, Beerbohm, and T. S. Eliot was formed to solicit contributions on his behalf.[83] On his eightieth birthday he was guest of honor at the Hungaria in the company of Beerbohm, Lady Benson, W. W. Jacobs, Augustus John, and other celebrated artists, where he was presented with a snug check.[84]

To supplement his pension, the old warrior put on his slightly tarnished armor and went to battle once more with the only weapon he possessed—the pen. He wrote book reviews and articles for such publications as *The American Mercury, The Bookman, Everyman, The Independent, John O'London's Weekly, The New Statesman, The Sunday Times, Theatre Arts,* and many others. Mr. T. Y. Horan of Dalton, Georgia, assisted him somewhat by buying a series of essays, written 1931 to 1934, to be published in book form. Because of the depression, however, Horan could not finance publication, and the book did not appear until after Machen's death under the title of *Bridles & Spurs.* In 1933 Benn published Machen's new novel *The Green Round,* a hodgepodge fantasy lacking continuity and verisimilitude. It combined dream psychology, alchemy, poltergeists, and other supernatural devices purportedly to show the role played by the newspapers in the creation of twentieth-century myth. The book was very unsuccessful.

In 1936, both *The Cosy Room* and *The Children of the Pool* appeared: the first, a collection of his old tales with the exception of "N"; the second, a collection of entirely new tales. Although none of the tales in the latter are exceptional and many are repetitive of earlier stories in style and theme, in "The Bright Boy" and in "The Tree of Life" Machen made some concession to the modern trend toward psychological thrillers. "The Bright Boy" deals with a pathological killer who lures a little girl into the forest only to be thwarted by her unexpected display of affection when he had expected horror and fear. "The Tree of Life" also has a surprise ending when it is revealed that the central character, who has a brilliant but twisted mind, has been residing throughout his lifetime, not in a country manor, but in a madhouse. During the 1920's Machen had written a few tales for Cynthia Asquith's anthologies, and the genre of the weird and occult was the field in which he remained creative.

After 1936, however, his literary career was almost at an end. He translated the annotations of the Sirène edition of Casanova's

Memoirs in 1938; and he edited *A Handy Dickens* in 1939. T. S. Eliot of Faber and Faber liked Machen's early horror stories and was sympathetic toward the Dickens project, but the firm said no.[85] Another company issued the work in 1941. Machen's last published book during his lifetime was *Holy Terrors* (1946), a collection of stories from earlier times, which sold over eighty thousand copies.[86] In 1946, he sold the film rights of *The Terror* to Emlyn Williams, who composed a film against its background the following year.[87]

As can be seen, Machen's literary output during these declining years was not significant either in volume or in merit. He had little work to do. One of the ways in which he spent his leisure was corresponding voluminously with new friends and old. He wrote literally thousands of letters, only a small fraction of which have been collected and about a hundred published. The main recipients during this period were Waite, Jepson, Stonor, Hillyer, Evans, Paul England, Gawsworth, and Howard Wolf; but he readily answered letters even from complete strangers with the utmost frankness. On July 1, 1936, for example, he explained to Miss Kurtz, who at one time contemplated writing his life, that Sylvia Townsend Warner was his niece by marriage and that he was no longer angry at Vincent Starrett for publishing *The Glorious Mystery* without first consulting him as to the selections included.

The remainder of Machen's leisure was consumed in a round of parties with boon companions, such as Evans, Holbrook Jackson, Augustus John, who did a portrait of him, and Tommy Earp, art critic of *The Daily Telegraph*. He also made new friends, notably Edwin Greenwood, a screen writer and author of mystery stories, as well as a neighbor of Machen; Norah Hoult, author; John Betjeman, poet; and during World War II, Mrs. C. A. Lejeune and her son Anthony. The war, however, left him on the sidelines as the younger generation became involved. Over the years, he had seen his old friends and acquaintances die off one by one—first, Francis J. Hudleston, his brother-in-law, in 1927; second, Jepson in 1938; then, Greenwood, 1939; Waite, 1942; M. P. Shiel, 1947; and finally his wife died on March 30, 1947. Machen's own death came soon after on December 15. Of the 1890's figures, only Shaw and Beerbohm outlived him. To perpetuate Machen's memory, the late Nathan van Patten, librarian and chief bibliographer of Stanford University, started the Arthur Machen Society, presently an expanding organization.

In perspective, one fact emerges with force and clarity: Machen had throughout his lifetime the inner urge and compulsion to write. To be sure, the preponderance of his work was performed under the stress of the necessity for earning a living; but, even under such circumstances, he displayed a remarkable freedom and independence, unhampered by the strictures of editorial policy. His *juvenilia* and translations, although unworthy of further consideration as consummate representations of creative art, nonetheless served as his apprenticeship to the trade and foreshadowed his development as a versatile and meticulous stylist.

Then followed the period of the 1890's during which he was, by virtue of financial security, free to create in his own fashion. The Wilde scandal, however, made publishers unusually chary. Even in the decade following, when Machen's major works came into print, the Aesthetic-Decadent school still had an unsavory quality which distorted critical opinion. Machen, therefore, turned to malicious and vituperative satire so outlandish as to place him as a forerunner of Mencken. Unfortunately, Machen was not in harmony with the movement of the times. He was fighting for the old traditions, not anticipating the new.

Not until time and life and journalism had mellowed him did Machen turn out a few more creative works which led to the discovery of all that he had done before. Undoubtedly the temper of the 1920's in the reckless search for values, the fads, the cults, the coteries, made possible Machen's brief burst of popularity. On the other hand, a reasonable deduction is that the works have some inherent worth dissociated from the era itself inasmuch as they were written with another age in the background and they were so strikingly opposed to realism, which was in the process of becoming the prevailing mode. After the early 1920's, except for an occasional tale in the genre of the weird and occult, Machen's creative efforts were negligible. He had to rely on repetition, reminiscences, or source material in order to write at all. In retrospect, then, a critical commentary must of necessity focus upon the works of the 1890's and upon the few works following which led to their discovery.

CHAPTER 2

The Ineffable Mystery

MACHEN, unlike most other creative writers, contributed a large number of strictly expository and argumentative essays to periodicals from 1898 onwards, and in these he explicitly stated his beliefs in areas vital to cultural development. Through an examination of some of his more penetrating ideas, a definite pattern can be formulated which, if not a comprehensive philosophy, is at least a decisive attitude toward life. The critical task of establishing literary influences and of examining the creative works with respect to genre, style, symbolism, and theme can thus be greatly simplified by eliminating the necessity for deducing these points implicitly from the works themselves.

Inasmuch as Machen was a commercial writer, the charge might be leveled that he was not sincere or that he was writing in conformance with editorial dictates. Such accusations could very well have some validity in the case of filler articles, book reviews, reportorial items, and advertising pamphlets; therefore such materials have been excluded from consideration in evaluating his attitudes as expressed in his writing. Certain featured articles, however, which Machen himself selected for book publication are less suspect, particularly when the same basic, dogmatic assertions are repeated many times. Further testimony to these opinions is found in his personal letters to friends, so that what follows is at least representative of the general tenor of his basic beliefs.

I *Education*

William Price Albrecht charged: "Machen is at home, we shall see, in the past, in himself, and in the land beyond sensation, but from the life about him, I am afraid, he has made a complete escape."[1] Such allegations are misinterpretations of Machen's defense of romance in literature. In actuality, his personal letters show that he was vitally concerned with temporal developments, but only with respect to their effect upon the eternal well-being of humanity.

As has already been mentioned, Machen noted as early as 1904 the changing emphasis in education. In fact, his much earlier experiences during his own school days were at least partially responsible for his not acquiring any more formal training than he did. Much of the scathing satire in *The Secret Glory* is directed at the decline of intellectual achievement, the promotion of athleticism, and the tendency toward crass commercialism in the schools. In this respect, he was by many decades ahead of Robert Hutchins and other critics of gladiatorial stables.

The early twentieth-century school laws had democratized education and broadened it to include the scientific and the technical. To these innovations Machen was categorically opposed and thus became a belated adversary of Huxley in the Arnold-Huxley controversy. Machen's pronouncement is almost identical to Arnold's: "Education is a mental and spiritual training; it has no relation of any sort to the matter of technical instruction. . . ." [2] Although pure science is generally accepted in the curriculum today as a method of developing the intellectual faculties, applied science and manual arts are dubiously educative in nature. The fallacy, as Machen was quick to see, is the inclusion of the technical with the developmental in the same school system to the detriment of both. His contention was that education is either for making a living or for developing intelligence, that we should do one or the other and not spoil good workmen and make bad scholars.[3] His feeling was that compulsory education has made man lower than badly behaved apes; the solution was to take children to High Mass and to see that they believe in fairies.[4]

Such statements leave no doubt that Machen conceived of education as a process in which only a select few could participate and that compulsory education for all, which arose from more democratic concepts, simply resulted in reducing the intellectual level of the few to that of the masses without appreciably raising the intellectual level of the many. Reduced to its basic proposition, Machen's argument reads like this: "The stubborn child who will not learn the alphabet, it is clear, shall neither read nor write immortal verse. . . ."[5]

Despite his lack of a higher education, he developed a tremendous respect for classical scholarship and humanistic values: "The Humanists, it may be conjectured, thought of school and University as places where Latin and Greek were to be learned, and to be learned with the object of enjoying the great thought and the great style of the antique world. One sees the spirit of this in Rabelais, for example. The Classics are a wonderful adventure; to learn to understand them is to be a spiritual Columbus, a discoverer of new seas and unknown continents, a drinker of new-old wine in a new-old land."[6]

Machen himself had mastered the art of scholarship. He had acquired over the years a vast knowledge of Dickens; of the medieval system; of occultism; of the French, Latin, and Welsh languages; of folklore; and of religion. One of the lasting interests of his life was the Holy Graal, which, for him, was the most satisfying symbol of faith; and through his research on the subject, he gratified his religious being and fulfilled the mystical qualities of his Celtic heritage. On this one subject alone, Machen felt that he was actually indulging in scholarship; and he wrote many articles for *The Academy* in 1907 and was even involved in a disputation with Alfred Nutt concerning the true nature and meaning of the Graal. Despite his studies, however, he believed that the secret of the Graal would always remain a mystery.[7] For his research and his treatises on the subject, he was not exactly joking when he asked Hillyer in a letter dated February 1, 1928, to try to get him an honorary degree.

Although Machen had enrolled his son in the classical curriculum at Merchant Taylors' School, he found modern methods much changed from those of his own childhood; and he found Education—the professed science of teaching people how to educate—to be wanting. In alluding to Casanova's early life, he wrote: "They 'brought them on' much more quickly in those days than in ours, when we gabble so much about the science of education that we have no time left for educating."[8] His utter detestation of modern education can be summed up in this epigraph: "Education increases; ignorance grows deeper."[9]

II *Politics*

Similarly, Machen was a traditionalist in politics, but decidedly no escapist. To him a more deadly foe than democracy was socialism. As early as 1907 he ridiculed the "New Shawrusalem" on the basis that wealth and happiness are not concomitant, that happiness is a process of spirit produced by some inward miracle and is beyond all social systems. He contended that true riches can be found only in refusing and renouncing.[10] Certainly, the man who, several years prior to World War I, saw the necessity of war as the only answer to international aggression was no escapist. He criticized most harshly an article in the *Daily Chronicle* which advocated disarmament when his country was in need of defense.[11]

With regard to economics, he felt that machines were enslaving modern man; [12] and his rebuttal to the materialistic claim that, under modern science and economy, the life span has been increased was cast rhetorically, "Does prolonging life do any good if happiness is no greater?" His answer is a simple spiritual declaration: "The new lamp may be of superior shape and elegance to the old; it will never summon the genie, it will never build the magical palace wherein the soul of man can dwell in peace and delight." [13] Machen, to be sure, was a meliorist; but he did not dwell in the past. He fought on an idealistic plane against all material changes instituted for their own sake; but on a practical level he accepted compromise or the nearest thing to his beliefs.

As he observed the changing social and economic structures throughout the world, Machen could find no system which corresponded completely with his idea of the "primal Paradise." His basic premise with regard to political and economic systems was the same that he applied to life itself: "You know that this difference is the source of most, if not all, of the joys & delights of life; in high things & in low. It is the sense of that that makes me the deadly foe of Protestantism, Democracy, & the standardised cooking of cosmopolitan hotels." [14] His own preferences, in other words, were medieval and lay in the unequal, yet ordered hierarchy of kings and priests, parsons and squires, in cosmos, not chaos.[15] Of the respective merits of monarchies and democracies, he could only say that the old system was good; the new, bad.[16] But, in practice, as he said in a letter of June 10, 1946, to Stonor, he was a political conservative, "I shall always vote for the blind-worm rather than the cobra."

On the basis of his deep-seated faith, he saw in atheistic Bolshevism from its earliest beginnings the enemy of civilization and humanity, an order which simply supported a greater population in squalor.[17] He was extremely intolerant of those who wanted to lower everyone to the level of the common dog and of those who pandered to the enemy of mankind, Communism. Furthermore, he saw that tolerance itself can be an evil when it takes the form of ignorance and indifference: "In a word, we are all extremely tolerant of persons whom we do not dislike and of opinions and actions to which we have no objection." [18]

In 1933, in reference to an economic conference which would provide money and trade for the Soviets, he stated that he would not put money into Russian hands because he did not like hands that are bloody and rebellious.[19] During the Spanish Civil War, contrary to the liberal movement at that time, Machen was quick to oppose the Communists: "Mr. A.M. presents his compliments and begs to inform that he is, and always has been, entirely for Gen. Franco." [20] As a deterrent to the Communist movement in Cleveland, Ohio, Machen suggested in 1939 to Cleveland columnist Howard Wolf that he read them the 38th Article of the Church of England: " 'The Riches and Goods of Christians are not common, as touching the right, title, and possession of the same, as certain Anabaptists do falsely boast.' " Opposing the strong world-wide body of Communist adherents of the 1930's, he wrote: "And there are certainly many influential quarters where it is held as an article outside debate that the cause of the Russian Soviets is the cause of freedom, as opposed to tyranny and reaction." [21] In 1946 his opinion was unchanged. In speaking of a news report from Russia of a cold winter, he said, "the occult doctrine of correspondences:—that which is without is that which is within." [22] To those who were cheered by the prospect of Communism, he had this to say, "but I am in accord with Huck Finn, in his comparison of snake bite and a draught of his father's whiskey: 'I'd ruther be bit by a rattle-snake myself.' " [23]

His solution to end all war, on the other hand, was to stick to games instead of the Russian experiment: "War will probably become unknown amongst peoples fully occupied with irrational, delightful, and absorbing pursuits. . . ." [24] When World War II was well under way, Machen noted to Howard Wolf (March 15, 1941) that he had prophesied the Fifth Column activities in 1918 in *The Terror.* His only apparent attempt to influence American neutrality was a reminder to his Cleveland correspondent, Wolf, (November 8, 1939) that if the United States entered the war, the Cleveland pacifists should remember the 37th Article: *Of the Civil Magistrates:* "'It is lawful for Christian men, at the commandment of the magistrate, to wear weapons, and serve in wars.'" Although his own son was in the war, Machen could still say to Evans (February 27, 1940) that war is an evil, but a sharp knife is better than putrefaction and death. At the end of the war, Machen further told Evans (October 11, 1945) that he was sent a peace ballot which he filled in by writing that he should be delighted to grow pineapples when Buckinghamshire became warmer. In the same letter he praised General Marshall as a man purged of illusions when the General said that we must keep ourselves strong.

In the field of international politics, Machen was not deluded by the prevailing faith in the United Nations as a panacea. He wrote to Evans (January 15, 1946) that the U.N. was wonderful, but the good will of the United States, Great Britain, and the Soviet Union were necessary if it were to be successful. Again, on the advent of atomic power, he wrote (August 9, 1945) that the split atom was not disastrous, despite the intimations of a fiery future; but again he reiterated that only cordial relations between the United States, the Soviet Union, and Great Britain can save the world from destruction.

Machen could never accept the Soviet position that the end justifies the means. Rather, he accepted the Jesuit position: "If your end is lawful, you will find that there is a lawful means of attaining it." [25] Yet, with all his hope and his struggle against the forces of evil, he had a devastating power of prophecy: "They [the Soviets] will be the Huns, Goths, & Vandals of a Decline & Fall far more horrible than the ruin chronicled by Gibbon." [26]

III *Science*

Albrecht strongly misstated the facts when he said of Machen: "He has no conception of the true scientist who penetrates the unknown to find mysteries at least as great as Machen's." [27] Such a statement is nonsense. Machen objected, it is true, to the scientific method; but his main criticism was of scientists who believe that their field of knowledge has the final answer. Of the real men of science, he contended that they realize that the greater man's knowledge, the more profound and illimitable becomes the mystery of the universe.[28] Although unschooled in the field of science and obviously not of the Huxley clan, Machen nevertheless had a faculty for pinpointing the inherent weaknesses of science as the ultimate answer to life's secret. The atomic theory, for example, once taught dogmatically in chemistry as the explanation of the fundamental nature of matter, can now be thought of as little more than an evolutionary step between the four elements of the ancient Greeks and the more modern concept of protons, electrons, positrons, neutrons, and any other smaller divisions of matter which the cyclotron may be capable of producing. By means of this marvelous new apparatus, man has now discovered the philosopher's stone, the main goal of the ancient alchemists; and the possibility now exists for transmuting all baser metals into gold, or anything into anything else, for that matter. Modern scientists speak of heavy hydrogen and of the isotopes of uranium, but are they not merely discovering that "H_2 is shorthand for ten distinct forces"? Machen could not create a *Brave New World* with all the authentic savor of the scientific jargon, but he always grasped immediately the implications of scientific innovations as far as the effect was concerned:

> We see shadows cast by reality. The more foolish of us gather up some of the shadows and put them in saucepans and boil them and then strain: and find out that water is really H_2O, which is true enough in its way, and will remain so: till it is found out that H_2 is shorthand for ten distinct forces, while O is a universe of countless stars, all revolving in their eternal orbit about an unknown, unconjecturable orb. And this, again, will be a good working hypothesis—till, new discoveries call for an entire revision of all our notions on the subject.[29]

For Machen, intimations were sufficient: "We see appearances and outward shows of things, symbols of all sorts; but we behold no essences, nor could we bear to behold them, if it were possible to do so."[30] No one can gaze with impunity on the fiery, mushroom-shaped cloud.

For Machen, science did not provide any of the answers. He

preferred to look to the past, "For tradition is always true." [31] His studies proved to him that the dragons of yesterday are the pterodactyls of today,[32] and the world has gained nothing and lost much in the renaming. He was quick to note that scientists cannot agree among themselves and that some even considered such persons as the inventors of the dirigible and the wireless to be mad. Aladdin's lamp, on the other hand, is perfectly conceivable.[33] Thinking, no doubt, of his own ailing liver and of his gout, Machen generalized that it is monstrous that science, mad in the abstract, should dictate to us in the concrete—that doctors who like meat and drink should advocate abstinence.[34]

During the 1920's when the temper was one of wild enthusiasms, Machen caught on among the occultists; and M. P. Shiel and Van Vechten professed to see in Machen's works hidden and esoteric meanings.[35] Machen was careful not to offend this body of readers; indeed, he offered them a definite rationale for their beliefs, though, as often as not, he was acting the role of an adept while secretly treating the whole matter as a delightful game. In fact, his works are studded with occult references that he picked up in the cataloging trade; and in a spirit of hoax he wrote several such documents himself—*A Chapter from the Book Called the Ingenious Gentleman Don Quijote de la Mancha, Thesaurus Incantatus,* and *The House of the Hidden Light.*

While his rebuttal to science did not lie in the direction of the occult arts, he often argued in their favor to annihilate the opposition. Thus he could say that the doctrines of occultism "may be a survival from the rites of the black swamp . . ." whence man first came or "an anticipation of a wisdom and knowledge that are to come, transcending all science of our day." [36] Although he conjectured that most of spiritualism can be brushed aside, he claimed, on the other hand, that no evidence shows that levitation is impossible.[37] He summed up his position by saying, "I do not understand the universe; consequently I do not dare to advance any such proposition." [38] He found no absolute negative answer to the question, "Does the impossible ever happen?" Experiences may be trifling, but they suggest more.[39] In other words, basically he was in harmony with Madame Blavatsky's dictum: "there is a logos in every mythos; or a ground-work of truth in every fiction." [40]

In spite of his tenderness for Madame Blavatsky, he thought

her a cheat[41] and her books humbug.[42] Likewise, he did not become a dupe as did his contemporary Conan Doyle, whose conversion, Machen maintained, would scarcely have been accepted by the Society of Psychical Research.[43] Nevertheless, though he rejected such exponents as Blavatsky and Hargrave Jennings, he could not, in view of his own beliefs, consistently refute the basic tenets of the Spiritualists or of the Rosicrucians who believe that the only reality is subjective and that anything is possible; so he accepted the intimations of the truth of the occult arts on the following basis: "if we are justified in disbelieving certain tales, though we have no logical grounds for our disbelief, so also we are justified in believing certain other tales, though we have no logical grounds for our belief." [44]

His sympathies, doubtless a product of his Celtic heritage, were therefore with occultism which sought—however mistakenly—to penetrate the unknown, as opposed to ordinary, not true, science which simply cataloged and renamed the known. But, just as he rejected the scientific method, so also he scorned any sect, group, or organized body of knowledge which professed to the attainment of ultimate truth. According to Albrecht, "He sees the spiritualist too certain of the mystery's solution and the scientist too certain of the lack of mystery. . . ." [45] With respect to the occultist peddlers, Machen had this to say: "It is as if these people had heard a rumour of something real from very far, had altogether misunderstood its meaning, had formalized its symbols into 'facts.'" [46] Still, he could, without straining his credulity, accept alchemical transmutations in a strictly subjective sense: "Like the old alchemists, we can truly say: 'The matter of our work is everywhere present.'" [47] Although he was undoubtedly familiar with the main treatises about every form of occultism, the test of his thinking on such matters was the list he selected for one of his correspondents to read: *Mysticism* by Evelyn Underhill, *The Grail* by Waite, and *Religio Poetae* by Coventry Patmore.[48]

He firmly maintained his position that science would lead us no closer to reality. His own supposition was that reality can never be found. It vanishes into the invisible conjectured land of electrons—manifestations of an eternal energy, part of the infinite cosmos.[49] Similarly, occult phenomena interested him only as symbols of forces beyond man's comprehension and beyond his power of solution. As Hillyer puts it: "His implied conclusion is, therefore, that no occult experience is of any consequence in itself; its sole value is to enhance the dignity, decency, and happiness of the human race." [50] To give life meaning, all fields of knowledge should have a common goal; in other words, method, or art, or science is simply concerned to restore the delights of the primal Paradise.[51]

IV *Religion*

Machen's male ancestors had all for several generations been clerics. His early childhood environment was a rectory, and his formal education was at a church school. Thus, seemingly, the principles of faith were a fundamental part of his nature. The truth, however, was that he rebelled from religion for a period during the 1880's and 1890's, as had his first wife, who had deserted the Roman Catholic Church. Nonetheless, on her deathbed, she returned to the fold. Machen himself, though he dabbled for a time in the occult arts, ultimately came to accept the faith of his father—Catholicism within the Anglican Church but tinged with Welsh mysticism. Though in certain circles some confusion existed at the time of Machen's death as to whether or not he had embraced Roman Catholicism, no real evidence has been presented to prove that he was ever anything other than a High Churchman.

For Puritanism in general and Protestantism in particular he had no use because he felt they were too immersed in the moral aspects of religion to leave room for faith. In other words, he contended that the end of Christianity is not morality. One should be good in order to be Christian, not the reverse.[52] Protestantism and Puritanism were abhorrent to him in the cold, practical application of moral principle which denied the beauties of mystical intuition and the pleasures of the flesh; and his lament was that the Reformation had ruined the church.[53] Actually, then, he was in most ways Catholic in his tolerance of fleshly pleasures, in his love of ritual sufficiently strange to accentuate the mystery of the bond between God and man, in his adherence to faith rather than to morals, and in his belief in the possibility of miracles. In religion, Machen accepted only that which seemed to give the widest scope for existence for all humanity. He was, therefore, able to laud the merits of Catholicism, yet attend the Anglican

Church; and, further, he was able to laud Anglicanism, but secretly adhere to Celtic sanctity and to the ancient Mass of the Britons.[54]

Any deviation from strict orthodoxy pointed toward misty Avalon rather than toward the dome of St. Peter's. In 1906 Machen had investigated the legend of the Graal in connection with the vanished Celtic Church of the fifth, sixth, and seventh centuries.[55] He concluded "that the Legend of the Graal" from romances "is the glorified version of early Celtic Sacramental Legends" married to myth and folklore, as opposed to political allegory, pagan survivals of sun heroes, or the Templar heresy.[56] Machen's conjecture was based upon the lives of the Welsh saints in which he detected the possibility of a Celtic liturgy differentiated from the Roman.[57] Furthermore, he felt that the Knights of Arthurian legend represented Welsh saints, that the Sacred Relic was confused with the pagan Magic Cauldron, that the ruin of the Celtic Church became "the desolate 'enchantment' of Britain," and that the death of Cadwaladr was the passing of Galahad.[58]

On the mystical side, Machen never lost faith that by some miracle Eden might be restored: "true miracles never contradict and defy nature; they rather restore nature to its first and unfallen state." [59] Machen's version of *Paradise Lost* is as follows:

> They say that man proceeds from that Great Deep (*pelagus vastissum*) which we call for convenience God, that he has fallen into the world of the senses, that all his poetry and his pictures and his emotion of exquisite and thrilling beauty and his tears at dawn and sunset and the joy of the dance and the happy laughter of lovers, that all these things are signs and recollections and memories of the Old Garden, whence he has come, whither he would return.[60]

On the expedient side, however, he did not practice austere asceticism while waiting for an apotheosis. He wrote much of the pleasures of food and drink and consumed on an even larger scale. Similarly, he would have preferred some ancient chapel, an earlier form of Mass, and a service in a strange tongue; but since the Established Church presented the best available expression of the mysteries, he felt bound to attend it.

V *Literature*

Machen's views on literature and art are lucidly and eloquently expressed in *Hieroglyphics,* a creative-critical work which will be fully evaluated later as one of his major productions. At this time, therefore, only his more general attitudes and notions will be considered, especially as they elucidate his own purposes and techniques and pass judgment on his qualifications as a writer.

Personally, except for Gothic architecture and religious music, he had little knowledge of the arts other than literature. He was no aesthete like George Moore. Yet, philosophically, he saw in the common aspirations of all artists that spirituality which distinguishes man from the beasts: "It is not by reason, as reason is commonly understood, that man is distinguished from the other animals; but by art." [61] Art he defined as "the love of splendour and the desire to create it" [62] and as "the expression of the human soul, of the eternal things in man; and to man it is as profoundly natural as is the song to the bird." [63]

Machen used the term "reason" to convey the ability to deal with practicalities, like buying the groceries, working out the budget, or washing the dishes. To man, he attributed a higher or transcendental faculty called "Reason," which was the basis for creative aspirations. Machen's version goes something like this: in the pristine period a mammal went mad and became man. "Man from the beginning has been perfectly irrational; that is, he has sought for God, and truth, and beauty, by the ways of religion, philosophy, and art." [64] This mothlike creature has invented various escapes from "business," which is not his true business. The best escape is that which leads farthest "from the prison of the body to the free lands of the spirit." [65] "Tom O'Bedlam's Song," like the poetry of Coleridge and Poe, is just such an escape into the desolate regions of the spirit. "And so with the journeys of the spirit; on these also there are wild and haggard and desolate places to be seen." [66]

The purpose of literature, therefore, in Machen's estimation, is to penetrate the surface realities and to seek out the eternal verities. This pursuit he assigned to romance, the office of which is to deal with reality, to unveil the truth.[67] Its task is to penetrate the outward show, to see London as Syon as Blake did, or as a goblin city as Dickens did. For as a great mystery of black depth and shining heights, "the whole world and sum of things, the spiritual world of men and all their works, disclose incredible but most veracious marvels to those who gaze on it in the spirit of romance." [68]

In this attitude, then, lies the basis for Machen's criticism of science, utilitarianism, and Naturalism: they normally deal with superficial realities. "For science is wholly of this world, but the arts communicate in their mysterious manner the secrets of that other world which lies beyond the vision of most of us. . . . For, you cannot have a blueprint of the light that never was on land or sea." Machen further says that art is not concerned with likenesses, and the great characters of fiction are the archetypes, humans the feeble copies: "These figures of Cervantes, Dickens, of the great romancers are of the very heart of life, of the real life which art reveals to us." [69] Of good sewage and cough lozenges, of the utilitarian faith of the modern world, he had this to say: "the wind in the trees, or the glitter of the brook, or a line of Keats will scatter it all away; and we awake from nightmare, and know that the well-being of the body is the means; the joys of the spirit the end." [70]

Machen, however, reserved his fiercest vituperation for denouncing Naturalism in literature. He castigated it as a product of the infernal atheism which insisted that to be art a book must be miserable. Although he conceded that literature has room for tragedy with redemption at the end, literature as a whole, he felt, should look forward to a good end. He deplored as a melancholy thing that the term "psychology" is applied only to the work of a "crazy Russian whose outlook on life is that of a melancholy madhouse, whose habit of life is verminous. . . . Atheism, vermin, skin disease, & melancholy madness are touchstones of art." [71] Unfortunately, one never finds out who the "crazy Russian" is. The description most appropriately fits Gorki's *The Lower Depths,* but Machen could very well have started to read *Crime and Punishment* and never finished it. At any rate, he never knowingly read a Russian author during his entire life; and this hopeless prejudice deprived him of some of the world's masterworks. In addition to Tolstoi, Dostoevski, and Chekhov, he berated Dreiser, Hecht, and Hemingway for their extreme realism. Oddly enough, *La Terre,* by Zola, the master of Naturalism, was one of Machen's favorites, though none of Zola's other works receives comment.

In Conrad's case, Machen admitted his own blindness; and, indeed, the author who writes of life in terms of enigmas and inscrutable mysteries should have been one of Machen's favorites; but he evidently read only Conrad's *Victory,* and that under the stress of financial pressures to write a commentary for George T. Keating's *A Conrad Memorial Library.*

In 1935, Machen took his last fling at the world of science, Grundyism, utilitarian principles, and the modern nastiness of the new barbaric and Naturalistic art. The essay, appropriately entitled "Farewell to Materialism," more or less ended his career where it began. It ridiculed the opposing forces and extolled the world "of sensible perishable things which both veil and reveal spiritual and living and eternal realities. . . ." [72]

On a more personal level, his own lack of success and his frustration in the artistic field gave him unusual insight into the creative process and made it possible for him to present a rational explanation of the peculiar psychosis of the literary mind which struggles for fulfillment against adverse circumstances, but remains perennially unfulfilled: "Yet, there is no denying the existence of this literary impulse; it is impossible to overlook its amazing strength and persistence in the face of every discouragement: poverty and hunger, sneers and jeers without; capital sentences of judgement within—and yet the man of letters, though he die daily, yet lives and renews his endeavour." [73] The artist's perpetual tragedy, therefore, and Machen's own, is the depth of the gulf between the idea and the word: "He dreamed in fire; he has worked in clay." [74]

In the declining years of his life, Machen wrote more from habit than from desire. Even in a year when he had most cause for jubilation, in 1925, he felt that, though he still hated the same things, his fighting spirit was gone.[75] This discouragement was not due to unfavorable criticism, which, by that time, he rather enjoyed, but to the realization that the masterpiece of his career was yet unwritten and that he now lacked the powers to produce it. Thus, when he wrote, "I have burnt my fingers to the bone again and again in the last forty years and I dread the fire of literature," [76] he was referring to his inability to give expression and meaning to an inner concept which he had carefully nurtured over the years. In his own opinion, he had laid a mine, pressed a button, and all that emerged was a feeble pop, "which would hardly make a kitten jump." [77] To him, his life had been blighted by a slight tinge of genius, a "juxtaposition of desire and impotence." [78] No fairer or more deeply considered evaluation of his limitations has yet been uttered.

VI *Philosophy*

Machen's knowledge of philosophy as a systematic body of thought was almost nil. He derived what he did know from Tennemann's *A Manual of the History of Philosophy,* from Coleridge, and from Plato. To classify Machen as a philosopher in the technical sense would, of course, be misleading; but, certainly, few writers composed such a large body of expository material which deals with life as a whole and which so far outweighs, in mass alone, the creative works. Machen's pronounced and dogmatic assertions of his convictions definitely establish his principles and attitudes; and the problem now is to reconcile the dabbler in occultism with the devout Anglo-Catholic, the introvert writer with the extrovert actor, the journalist and hack with the independent creative thinker, and the man of the flesh with the man of the spirit.

To begin with, Machen frequently and explicitly acknowledges his reverence for Plato. Although Machen does not speak of Forms or Ideas, he consistently adheres to "higher realities," by which he doubtless means much the same thing. Machen, however, appears to deviate somewhat from Plato's conceptual Realism when he considers the question of outer realities. He says that the real pattern of life is not apparent on the surface;[79] that our world is perhaps a dream of "the Supreme Artist";[80] that life is unreal, "a play within a play":[81] "And so I say that there is no such entity as the thing in itself, there is no absolute existence in things seen." [82] "No; we see nothing at all; though poets catch strange glimpses of reality, now and then, out of the corners of their eyes." [83]

The statement that the world is but an idea in the mind of God parallels very closely the subjective Idealist position, so Machen here is obviously speaking in literary terms rather than philosophical ones inasmuch as he could not be a Realist and an Idealist at the same time. The other statements above are more in conformance to a view of external reality from Plato's cavern. The conclusion, then, is irrevocable that Machen was not vitally concerned with a theory of knowledge or with metaphysical speculation. Just as he was unwilling to embrace or reject occultism, so he was unwilling to accept or deny either of the two fundamental philosophic concepts. He refused to niggle over terms.

His eclecticism, in fact, encompassed any or all philosophies which emphasized the spiritual and the mystic. His mind remained clear almost to the end of his life; and, notwithstanding his somewhat shallow opinions in certain fields, he maintained always the clear perspective of man seeking his higher destiny. He tried always to clear his own mind of cant,[84] and he was never untrue to his convictions. All of his life he opposed that type of rationalism which drags man back to bestiality;[85] and to Machen —the anti-Realist, the anti-Materialist, the anti-Aristotelian—all science was a lie.[86] It was in Coleridge's "Reason," a transcendental faculty, that he found his battle song against rationalism. Thus Coleridge's Kantian philosophy combined with Machen's innate Welsh mysticism to formulate the belief that the world is a world of symbols, "of sensible perishable things which both veil and reveal spiritual and living and eternal realities; and that order and reason (in the high significance which Coleridge gave the word), not disorder and nonsense, are the end and crown of all." [87]

But Machen was only a Transcendentalist in part; the other part was mystic. A brief summary of the basic propositions in Evelyn Underhill's *Mysticism,* which Machen endorsed without reservation and which he may have edited unofficially, will serve to illuminate his beliefs. Underhill's basic tenet is that all philosophies—even Idealism, which is the most sublime theory of Being —fail to find in practice their exclusive intellectual realities and that only the mystic is capable of immediate communion with the One Reality.[88] This union is achieved by means of an intuitive faculty in man—one divorced from emotion, intellect, and will— which lies below the threshold of consciousness and which can emerge through contemplation and other processes of the mystic, such as asceticism and self-hypnotism.[89] Whereas Transcendental philosophy is purely academic, mysticism is practical. It is a science of ultimates, of the union with the Absolute—not to know about but to Be.[90]

Just as Machen was not a systematic philosopher, so he was not a practicing occultist or mystic in any serious sense. He adopted a very practical point of view concerned only with the effect of philosophy on man's heritage. His approach was humanistic. On the one hand, he could detect that rationalism, determinism, and the materialism of Marx led only to a kind of hopeless and godless form of art called Naturalism; and on the other hand, Idealism and Transcendentalism produced works abounding in faith, mystery, and joy in life. In the social sense, he considered the example of Alexandria in the period of dissolution brought about by fleshly revel. He conjectured that the downfall of Alexandria lay not in paganism or in lack of morals, but in "decorated materialism." When revel becomes self-conscious, when people force themselves to drink "dubious whiskey in England and not dubious in America," then failure is imminent. The only objection to the Alexandrian way of life was that it did not work.[91]

Frequently, he took a deliberately perverse stand in order to bait Puritans and prigs. In "Rouge et Noir—and the Unknown," he defends gambling on the grounds that man is either supra-rational or infra-rational. He contends that "our vices and follies come from the same stock as do our gifts and graces. . . ." In this light, gambling therefore becomes the poetry of the unimaginative man because, basically, the delight of life lies in its uncertainty. Man has a vision of wonders—"all desire, few attain." Temperance and anti-betting leagues are thus doomed to failure because they are acting contrary to the fundamental nature of man. The imaginative faculty must have an outlet.[92]

Though Machen was a master logician, he did not spend his time developing an organized system of metaphysics or ethics. He did, however, as shown above, have organized values and a patterned attitude toward life. Despite the fact that Machen and Mencken were often attacking the same ossified ideas and outmoded thinking, Mencken, the iconoclast, tended to enjoy the process of destruction for its own sake without even providing new seedlings for a regrowth. In contrast, Machen merely trimmed the forest of its dead wood, never destroying an old oak just because it was old, provided its trunk was sound and solid. Where Mencken struck about wildly, Machen was selective. Where Mencken left it to the future to provide the necessary solution, Machen carefully sorted and sifted the past for cherished traditions of humanistic and spiritual value. Machen could never tolerate purely material changes made in the name of progress. He saw always another world beneath the outward form of matter. His artistic credo crystallized in the expression, "We live and move in a world of profound and ineffable mystery. . . ." [93]

In the twentieth century, the Idealist has tended to become isolated in his struggle against the encroachment of mechanization and industrialization. Thus in the 1920's Machen became the symbol of belated Romanticism and eccentric conservatism. Temporarily, at least, Mencken has won, but on a spiritual level the schism between barbarity and spirituality remains a perennial one to be fought out by each succeeding generation.

CHAPTER 3

The Necromancers

THE previous chapters on the life, minor works, and ideas of Machen suggest possible literary influences and associations and reveal clearly that his life was devoted to the cause of spirituality as opposed to rationality. In conformance to this principle, he believed that all literature should be a superior magic containing hints of otherworldliness. Many of his expository works are written as a defense of romance; his satires flay those opposed to it; and his creative works are all written in the same spirit to hint at the greater truths beyond the veil of sensible appearances. Furthermore, his eclectic philosophy was an amalgam of those systems of thought which conceded the supremacy of an intuitive or transcendental faculty by means of which man is enabled to penetrate the outward show of matter to the ineffable regions beyond. The creative artist, in order to convey the mystery, must of necessity rely upon symbols. Finally, in Machen's case, many of these were of an occult nature. This portion of the study therefore deals with the literary traditions and influences of the three pervading elements of his works—Romanticism, Symbolism and Mysticism, and weird and occult—so that, ultimately, complete elucidation of his major works can be accomplished.

I *Romanticism*

As might be expected of a thoroughgoing Romantic, Machen relied heavily for his source material and allusions upon three periods—the Medieval, the Romantic, and the later Victorian. Not so logical are his affiliations with the early Stuart writers. When the history of English literature is viewed in the light of convention and revolt, however, the truth becomes self-evident that succeeding ages alternate between the microcosm and the macrocosm, between facing the world of reality and withdrawing from it. When viewed in this context, the relationship between the early Stuart period and the others mentioned above at once becomes more reasonable. What binds them all together is a sense of withdrawal: withdrawal into religion, into the realm of pure imagination and pure art, and into the speculative and philosophical. Machen's aversion to the ages of Materialism, Rationalism, and outward expansion—the Elizabethan, the Pseudoclassic, the Victorian, and the twentieth-century Realistic and Naturalistic movement—thus takes on some meaning. Even his satire was not Pseudoclassic. It had one purpose—to ridicule the anti-spiritualists in order to prove by negation the eternal verities of Plato.[1]

In several superficial ways Machen utilized his knowledge of Medievalism. The underlying framework of many of his expository works is scholastic logic, which survived from the early trivium as an essential phase of the curriculum of the English schools, even as late as the twentieth century. Although Machen never used the conventional machinery of the Gothic novelist, he had the opportunity to study firsthand much of the surviving architecture of the Middle Ages, using as his guide Parker's *Glossary of Gothic Architecture*.[2] In an oblique way, Machen often utilized his knowledge in this field in such a manner as to display his contempt for the modern material standards characterized by an obliviousness to the glories of the past.[3] In addition, Machen traced the history of the Church back to its earliest origins and approached the Middle Ages through a scholarly admixture of history and legend. Besides these random allusions, Machen relied heavily for his source material upon *The Mabinogion* and upon Malory's *Morte d'Arthur*. "Guinevere and Lancelot" in *Notes and Queries* retells the story of these immortal lovers with touches of apocrypha added. Despite his avid interest in the period, only one of his works, *The Chronicle of Clemendy*, already discussed, is predominantly medieval, with archaic diction, knights and ladies, castles, and other appropriate paraphernalia.

Machen shared with Romantics Coleridge and Lamb a common respect and reverence for the great seventeenth-century stylists. In a speculative sense, he was more often concerned with such problems as what songs the sirens sang and with the causes and cures of melancholy than he was with material questions of his own day. Just as Lamb, in his imitative stage, wrote an exercise called "On the Melancholy of Tailors" to occupy his mind and elude the madness that beset him, so Machen in *The Anatomy of Tobacco* imitated Burton in order to escape the loneliness and privation of his early life in London. Machen admitted that his book was simply "easy schoolboy scholarship." [4]

With each of the writers of the Romantic period, Machen had much in common. He wrote *Hieroglyphics* in the manner of Coleridge's *Table Talk*.[5] His critical criterion is decidely subjective in its definition and, therefore, falls into the pattern established by Coleridge, Lamb, and De Quincey. The very thesis itself is an attempt to set up standards for the segregation of greater from lesser works of literature and is really an elaborate parallel of De Quincey's "The Literature of Knowledge and the Literature of Power."

Machen was, like Wordsworth, essentially a lover of nature; and, even setting aside their common mystical propensities, their methods of dealing with nature and its influence upon them were very similar. In "Beneath the Barley" Machen describes as the origin of his impulse toward literature an indelible scene from which arose an indescribable emotion—a pure and radiant blue mountain under a paler blue sky and white farmhouses looking as if they were marble in the direct sunlight. Two elements—first, emotion; second, the influence of nature on the soul of man—are characteristically Romantic and typically Wordsworthian. Also Machen makes frequent mention of Wordsworth's "Ode," and he seems to be summarizing the famous stanza beginning "Our birth is but a sleep and a forgetting" when he states that "experience causes us to forget most things that are worth knowing." [6] Even more remarkable is the similarity of purpose of Machen and Wordsworth. Of Wordsworth's motives, Coleridge gives the following account:

> Mr. Wordsworth, on the other hand, was to propose to himself as his object, to give the charm of novelty to things of every day, and to excite a feeling analogous to the supernatural, by awakening the mind's attention to the lethargy of custom, and directing it to the loveliness and the wonders of the world before us; an inexhaustible treasure, but for which, in consequence of the film of familiarity and selfish solicitude we have eyes, yet see not, ears that hear not, and hearts that neither feel nor understand.[7]

In many of his works Machen attempted to do in prose what Wordsworth was trying to do in his poetry, particularly with regard to revealing the wonders and the supernatural implications in common things. In his own words, "London will turn into Bagdad in an instant: if you have the true wand of transmutation." [8]

Machen, though he was no poet himself, regarded Coleridge's supernatural poetry very highly when he termed it "the vital truth," [9] and he indicated the magnitude of his affinity for Keats by the frequency of repetition of well-known quotations from his poetry. Despite Machen's complete spiritual empathy with the works of these poets, the correspondence in subject matter is negligible. The single idea of the snake woman personified by Helen Vaughan in *The Great God Pan* might be credited to Keats' "Lamia" and to Coleridge's "Christobel" or to their common source, Sir Thomas Browne's *Hydriotaphia.*

Machen's essays are too diverse in nature to trace to a single origin. One volume, however, called *Dog and Duck* has sufficient unity of style and subject matter to show several parallels with the works of Charles Lamb. In both, the choice of topics always tends toward the odd and the ancient with emphasis upon the human element involved; the same quaint effect produced by occasional archaisms and superfluous Latin tags is in each; and the net product of both writers is the illusion of antiquity. Machen, however, seldom emphasizes the feeling of pathos which is one of Lamb's obvious romantic tendencies.

The most pervasive romantic influence came to Machen, oddly enough, not from the English writers, but from Edgar Allan Poe, who also was the primal source allying Machen to the French Symbolist and the Aesthetic-Decadent movements, the manifestations of which will be considered later. Insofar as the present topic of consideration is concerned, however, Poe represents the bridge between Coleridge and Walter Pater. In *Biographia Literaria* Coleridge states that, though pleasure may be the immediate purpose of a literary work, "truth, either moral or intellectual, ought to be the ultimate end. . ." [10] and, further, that "the communication of pleasure is the introductory means by which alone the poet must expect to moralize his readers." [11] Poe, despite his great reverence for Coleridge, disavows the dictum that poetry need communicate something other than pleasure.[12] Writing "a poem simply for the poem's sake" became in Pater the creation of "art for art's sake." Thus the doctrine of the heresy of the didactic was broadened to include both poetry and prose; and at this point Machen turned it into a hue and cry against Puritanism.

Both Machen and Poe were preoccupied with the rhythmical creation of beauty but in different ways. To Machen, perhaps rationalizing his inability to write poetry, no distinction was apparent between poetry and prose. Therefore he created with an ear attuned to chant and incantation: "Language, he understood, was chiefly important for the beauty of its sounds, by its possession of words resonant, glorious to the ear, by its capacity, when exquisitely arranged, of suggesting wonderful and indefinable impressions, perhaps more ravishing and farther removed from the domain of strict thought than the impressions excited by music itself." [13] At any rate, Beauty, not quite in Poe's case the same Beauty which Keats held to be synonymous with Truth,[14] was the mutual basis for much of their thinking. Their beliefs were in concord on the unattainability of Beauty, which Machen expresses as "the desire of the moth for the star: the desire that ends in fiery torment." [15] The complete thought of this passage may best be revealed by reference to the source, Poe's "Poetic Principle": "We have still a thirst unquenchable, to allay which he has not shown us the crystal springs. This thirst belongs to the immortality of Man. It is at once a consequence and an indication of his perennial existence. It is the desire of the moth for the star. It is no mere appreciation of the Beauty before us—but a wild effort to reach the Beauty above." [16]

Beyond the similarity of their beliefs on some of the basic factors underlying the nature of art, several random and uncorrelated influences of Poe upon Machen may be mentioned in passing. In *Hieroglyphics* Machen uses the term "ecstasy" to denote the distinguishing quality of fine literature. The word is by no means uncommon; but Poe accentuates it in "Between Wakefulness and Sleep" by frequent repetition in a very short passage which contains Machen's conception of the purpose of art in embryo: "I regard the visions, even as they arise, with an awe which, in some measure, moderates or tranquilizes the ecstasy—I so regard them, through a conviction (which seems a portion of the ecstasy itself) that this ecstasy, in itself, is of a character supernal to the

Human Nature—is a glimpse of the spirit's outer world. . . . It is as if the five senses were supplanted by five myriad others alien to mortality." [17]

Another similarity in the works of Poe and Machen which is more than coincidental is the use of the omniscient sleuth who is able to solve all the most baffling enigmas of mankind without moving from his armchair. Machen's Dyson is very close to Poe's Dupin. A third striking parallel lies in the very nature of some of the tales themselves. Both writers have a large body of work which may be classified as terror stories, and both rely upon the power of suggestion and upon atmospheric detail to produce the required effect.

Poe, then, may be considered a focal point from which to work either backward to Coleridge and the Romantics, to include the Gothic, or forward to the Aesthetics of the "art for art's sake" group as well as to the French Symbolists. Machen might well have derived all the elements of his work which have just been considered from secondary sources of his own period; but that he did not is shown by his frequent tribute to Poe, whom he calls "the supreme realist" and "The Columbus of the spirit." Of "To Helen" and "The Fall of the House of Usher," Machen writes, "they mirror in forms beautiful and terrible the secret and innermost core of man's being." [18] He goes on to say, "in the achievement of E. A. Poe there is the quickening spirit, the sense of eternal reality and truth and beauty";[19] and with these words he not only pays his highest acclaim by attributing to Poe's works those qualities which he believed to be present exclusively in fine literature, but also reflects, at the same time, the standards in accordance with which he was endeavoring to create.

Another great writer, this time a contemporary, from whom Machen admittedly took lessons was Robert Louis Stevenson. In conscious conformity with the idea of Stevenson that places demand a story, Machen explained the origin of *The Great God Pan* as being a lonely white house on the top of a hill.[20] As Stevenson put it: "One thing in life calls for another; there is a fitness in events and places. . . . Certain dank gardens cry aloud for murder; certain old houses demand to be haunted; certain coasts are set apart for shipwreck." [21] Furthermore, just as Stevenson felt that the true significance of life was hidden "to one who has not the secret of the lanterns . . . ," [22] so Machen reaffirmed that the real pattern of life "lurks, half hidden, only apparent in certain rare lights, and then only to the prepared eye. . . ." [23] To discover reality, one must turn to romance.[24] As a consequence, since the views of both writers were in direct opposition to the theories of the Naturalists, Stevenson belittled the English Realists, the French "meat-market of middle-aged sensuality," and Tolstoi's *Powers of Darkness*.[25] For exactly the same reason Machen could not tolerate the naturalism of Arnold Bennett, Flaubert, or anything Slavonic, which he considered abominable[26] because the hidden truth is far removed from the outward show.[27]

Along with this ideological affinity, Machen played the sedulous ape in patterning his *Three Impostors* after *The New Arabian Nights*. When asked if his tales had any *fundamentum in re*, Machen replied in mock dignity that they came entirely from his head and Stevenson's.[28] In fact, "The Lost Club" in *The Cosy Room* is only slightly more than a replica of Stevenson's "Suicide Club" with little invention of its own. In addition to structural and conceptual similarities, the stylistic qualities bear a conscious resemblance. After 1895, however, he used "no more . . . rounded Stevensonian cadence." [29]

One of the prominent movements of the 1890's is the variously named "art for art's sake," Aesthetic, or Escapist trend that, in its incipient form is widely attributed to Pater. In a letter Machen makes a detailed analysis of his estimate of Pater's works, which he venerated by rumor but found boring on investigation. Admitting that *Marius* contained some beautiful passages, Machen nonetheless found the essay "Style" to be arid and uninspired. Still, in speaking of Pater's statement that the arts must be at last referred to the standard of music, Machen concedes that Pater must have the "root of the matter" in him, provided his meaning was that the arts must address the soul or spirit rather than the logical understanding. Machen then states that Mallock and Wilde both sat at Pater's feet and that Pater created the "Aesthetic" movement. Machen concludes, however, that the value of the products of this movement, which emanated from Pater and the Pre-Raphaelites, was very slight.[30]

Although this apparent disinterest would seem to belie all comparison, the statement of basic philosophy found in Machen's *London Adventure*—"Strangeness which is the essence of beauty is the essence of truth, and the essence of the world" [31]—has a point in common with the idea in Pater's Postscript to *Appreciations:* "It is the addition of strangeness to beauty, that constitutes the romantic character in art. . . ." [32] At least, if the latter statement is correct. Machen's affiliation with the Romantic cause at once becomes obvious.

Again, in the following passage from the conclusion to *The Renaissance,* Pater seems to have expressed the basic creed of a group of writers of the 1890's: "Every one of those impressions is the impression of the individual in his isolation, each mind keeping as a solitary prisoner its own dream of a world." [33] This heavy emphasis upon the subjective and the particular manner of its expression might almost be considered Machen's *Hill of Dreams* in embryo. In this and subsequent passages Pater unwittingly gave expression to the conscious manifestations of hedonism, epicureanism, escapism, and sensationalism which form an integral part of the literature of this period. Of these phases of aestheticism, the one most frequently charged against Machen is that of escapism. His critical work, *Hieroglyphics,* drew adverse criticism for its dichotomy of Romanticism and Realism and for the implied separation of art and life. Against the imputation that escapism invalidates art, he created a standard defense which contains, as well, the elements of a counterattack:

> But this curse of getting a livelihood remains profoundly unnatural to man, in spite of his long experience of it: hence his frantic efforts to escape from what he erroneously calls life by running himself red in the face at Lord's, by rowing himself blue in the face at Henley, by drinking methylated spirit, by "putting on" those criminal bobs, by playing mind-torturing games like chess, by knocking small balls into small holes, by climbing Alps—and even by writing books.[34]

But to turn once more to Pater, the history of the later Victorian period in literature reveals that his mild glorification of sensation at any given moment led the way—hand in hand with the *Rubaiyat*—to the sensationalism of Rossetti, Swinburne, Symons, and Wilde; to the cult of the prostitute; to the devastation of morals; to the separation of ethics and art; to the school of decadence. The extent to which Machen participated in this movement can only be determined by a detailed analysis of the individual works, but publication of his *The Great God Pan* and *The Three Impos-*

tors by John Lane gave the reviewers sufficient cause to label them as shockers and as cheap pieces of sensationalism. Machen's fundamental association with the members of this group lay in the common belief in the heresy of the didactic: "Literature, he knew, could not exist without some meaning, and considerations of right and wrong were to a certain extent inseparable from the conception of life, but to insist on ethics as the chief interest of the human pageant was surely absurd." [35] This absurdity of insisting on a moral, which had been a puritanical Victorian propensity, he satirized vehemently and in mock deference attached a ludicrous moral to some of his own stories.[36]

Thus, despite his professed aversion to Pater, Machen assimilated a considerable number of Pater's basic ideas either by direct syphoning or by indirect osmosis. With the other notable writers of the later Victorian period, however, his only direct contact of significance was with Wilde; and, though Machen apparently read such works as *Salome* and *The Picture of Dorian Gray,* his account of the meetings with Wilde shows the vast breach between his manner of thinking and that of his notorious contemporary. Yet, despite the general disparity of mediums, styles, and ways of life, the larger elements of decadence—intent to shock, emphasis on sensation, and fascination with evil—are common bonds. Thus, though Machen, in 1915, considered himself to be "not even a small part, but no part at all" [37] of the 1890's, the evidence is conclusive that, no matter how independent he felt himself to be, he was still somewhat a product of his age.

Historically speaking, Richard Le Gallienne draws the writers of this period together in the following manner: "I have called the '90's 'romantic' . . . because their representative writers and artists emphasized the modern determination to escape from the deadening thraldom of materialism and outworn conventions, and to live life significantly—keenly and beautifully, personally and, if need be, daringly; to win from it its fullest satisfactions, its deepest and richest and most exhilarating experiences." [38] The spirit of revolt which links all these individuals together is the same that incited the earlier and more productive Romantic movement, but in the intervening sixty years the cultural milieu had radically altered. As a result, some of the literary productions became formless, others were experimental, and many exhibited a distinct taint.

II *Mysticism and Symbolism*

In a philosophical sense, the Romantic is always attempting to convey hints of the dream world which has existence only in imagination or fancy, in the ideal world, or in the world of supernaturalism. To paraphrase the words of Coleridge, the Romantic may attempt to excite the feeling of the supernatural from the events of ordinary life; or he may start with purely imaginative material and attempt to render it credible or to give it the air of reality.[39] Thus, the alliance of the Romantics with the Idealistic, Transcendental, and Mystical philosophers—Plato, Berkeley, Kant, Swedenborg—becomes clearly explicable; and Mysticism and Symbolism become the extreme manifestations of the Romantic impulse in its broadest application: in the sense of the subjective as opposed to the objective.

The Realist, on the other hand, is deterministic and materialistic in his beliefs. Though he may, at times, use such symbols as "Pride," "Prejudice," and "Vanity Fair," they only serve the purpose of revealing the state of this world and not of hinting at the mysteries of the next.

Machen was Romantic in the all-inclusive sense, both in philosophy and technique; and he used—in common with Poe, Hawthorne, Wordsworth, Blake, Keats, Coleridge, and De Quincey—mystical and symbolic language to convey those higher truths which cannot be apprehended by sensory means and which cannot be proved by logic alone. He stood upon the principle of something hidden beneath the surface: "We pass through, we perceive sensibly, temporal things in order that we may gain eternal things, the everlasting essences that are at once hidden in the visible and tangible and audible universe and communicated by it." [40] Artistically, he felt: "He does best who hints most closely at the secret message latent in the signs exhibited to us." [41] A rapid survey of the periods upon which Machen drew for his inspiration places his mystical and symbolistic leanings in the perspective of the literary tradition.

Though Machen had studied St. Augustine's *City of God,* he did not draw strongly upon the medieval period for symbols. Rather, he drew for his inspiration upon the *Song of Songs,* upon the font of the Holy Church itself, upon the period when the Great Errantry merged with Christianity, and upon the pagan times and the primordial past. In the sense of loss in the Graal legend, he envisioned once more the original fall. The search for restoration and grace became embodied in the Holy Cup of Teilo Sant and led Machen backward in point of time to the misty borderland between the Christian and pagan eras before faith became dogma and before man's worship became fixed ritual: "We can hardly conceive, perhaps, how in the Dark Ages man lived in a world of mystery and love and adoration, how sacraments stood about all his ways, how the Veil of the Temple grew thin before his gaze, and he saw the Great Sacrifice offered in the Holy Place." [42] All of Machen's symbols have a foundation in Welsh history and folklore, and all are peculiarly his own.

Likewise, the seventeenth century provided him with few literary sources of a mystical nature. To be sure, he had read Traherne, but Machen achieved felicity not so much by returning to a state of childhood as by regaining ancestral consciousness. The Vaughan he read was not Henry the "Silurist," but his brother Thomas, who wrote occult, alchemical treatises. Like Crashaw, Machen was a mystic of flame, but there the resemblance ends. The total absence of derivative influence from a period which he revered and which molded his style emphasizes the loneliness of the mystic and the individual nature of Symbolism.

The mystic, like the prophet, stands alone. He gets his inspiration from God alone and acknowledges no man as his teacher. The most solitary figure in English literature is William Blake, and Machen's works reflect much the same detachment from humanity. Machen's concern was, as Krutch says, "exclusively with transcendental Sin and transcendental Virtue—not with particular sins or particular virtues which, as James realized, have a way of turning out to be disappointingly petty, but with Good and Evil themselves, considered as the only mystic realities." [43] Blake saw them as natural complements, but Machen wrote of them in two separate and distinct manners: "All his villains are Fausts, taking supernal knowledge by storm; all his heroes Blakes, gazing mildly at the tree full of angels and harkening to the chant of the morning sun." [44] For sorcery, he relied to a considerable extent upon weird and occult devices and upon pagan symbols; and for sanctity, he reserved liturgical rhythms and Christian symbols. On a common plane, however, the basic premise of Mysticism is always the same. Blake stated it thus:

To see a World in a Grain of Sand,
And a Heaven in a Wild Flower.
Hold Infinity in the palm of your hand,
And Eternity in an hour.[45]

To Machen, the essence of the mystic view was summed up in the statement of Oswald Crollius, " 'In every grain of wheat there lies hidden the soul of a star.' " Not quite content, however, with this classic aphorism, Machen elaborated that within the grain of wheat were worlds on worlds, made after the similitude of the starry heavens, the electrons moving round their suns in ceaseless motion and eternal, inevitable order.[46] As Krutch put it, Machen had "only one theme, the Mystic Vision, and only one plot, the Rending of the Veil." [47]

With two later writers, Machen's affiliations were less tenuous. He was peering "as Poe and Hawthorne peered, into the places of thick darkness, and, above all, voyaging into the unknown, perpetually climbing the steep white track that vanishes over the hill." [48] Machen felt that Hawthorne was a conscious mystic[49] and expressed reverence for his works, but the similarities in style do not go beyond a general remoteness which tends toward the shadowy and unreal side of life. Their differing symbols, nonetheless, are drawn from the folklore and history of their respective countries, America and Wales.

With Poe, on the other hand, the association is more direct, a fact which also explains some of the similarities between Machen's works and those of the French Symbolists. As Turquet-Milnes points out, Poe was one of the chief authors instrumental in bringing the Symbolist spirit to England;[50] and Poe was next to Dickens, Cervantes, and Rabelais on Machen's list of favorite authors. Machen felt Dupin to be "a symbol of the mystagogue." [51] The dwarfish little man who dogs Hillyer's footsteps in *The Green Round* is a close parallel to the shadowy double or conscience in "William Wilson." The idea of lurking, omnipresent, timeless evil which Poe expresses in "The Man of the Crowd" is expressed by Machen through the symbol of the Little People. The prose medium most readily adaptable to the requirements of mysticism is fantasy, and both authors are adept in that field. The concepts of the alter ego and of the interpenetration of one age by another, though not the exclusive property of the mystic, certainly tend to conform to the pattern of his beliefs; and both authors, again, deal with these subjects. The use of the prose poem to express momentary visions of rapport and communion is also a bond between them, as it is between Baudelaire and Rimbaud and De Quincey. Altogether, the resemblances between the works of Poe and Machen are too strong to be termed merely coincidental.

Notwithstanding the fact that Machen was indisputably Romantic in major phases of his work, the Romantic period in England yielded little to him structurally or ideologically as far as the mystical and symbolic aspects were concerned. Coleridge and Shelley were using what might be called systematic symbolism in "The Ancient Mariner" and "Prometheus Unbound," respectively; but Machen mainly used random symbols as they occurred to him to express some hidden meaning. In other words, the context was not made to be solely reliant upon the symbolism. Machen was more in sympathy with the suggestive phrases of Keats which, by virtue of their apt usage, have become symbols of the awe, the wonder, and the mystery of the universe.[52] Similarly, Machen repeatedly extolled Wordsworth's "Ode on Intimations of Immortality" as the epitome of mystical perfection in expressing the inexpressible. As far as mysticism and symbolism are concerned, however, the English Romantics offered nothing in the way of style, material, or literary medium that he thought worth borrowing, despite his unqualified admiration for their best works in these fields.

Neither can it be said that Machen was following the precepts of his contemporaries. The Celtic spirit was an element of English literature as early as Spenser's day and even before that appeared in Malory and in *Sir Gawain and the Green Knight.* The writer most nearly contemporary, whose works parallel Machen's in the feeling of mystical rapport transmitted through cadenced prose, was Pater; and, just as some of Machen's nuclear ideas regarding Romanticism are embodied in Pater's works, so also, certain mystical passages, particularly those dealing with the effect of music and religious ritual upon the soul, bear remarkable resemblance. Either of the following passages from Pater could find a place in Machen's *Secret Glory* or *A Fragment of Life:*

So he yielded himself easily to religious impressions, and with a kind of mystical appetite for sacred things; the more as they came to him through a saintly person who loved him tenderly, and believed that this early pre-occupation with them already marked the child out for a saint. He began to love, for their own sakes, church lights, holy days, all that belonged to the comely order of the sanctuary, the secrets of its white linen, and holy vessels, and fonts of pure water; and its hieratic purity and simplicity became the type of something he desired always to have about him in actual life.[53]

The religious poetry of those Hebrew psalms—*Benedixisti Domine terram tuam: Dixit Dominus Domino meo, sede a dextris meis*—was certainly in marvellous accord with the lyrical instinct of his own character. These august hymns, he thought, must thereafter ever remain by him as among the well-tested powers in things to soothe and fortify the soul.[54]

Similarly, Machen had certain nonderivative common traits with the French Symbolists. He stood far afield, as they did, from realism, naturalism, and sheer rhetoric. They were mutual defenders of the spiritual cause. Fortified by the pillars of Catholicism, the French Symbolists made occasional forays into the realm of Satan, usually returning unvictorious to the fold to seek sanctity. In "The White People" Machen's images taken from Roman and Welsh mythology are decidedly far removed from the naked, catlike body of the octoroon Jeanne Duval, who was Baudelaire's particular demon and ideal of beauty; yet the principle is the same. Machen rebelled intellectually; the French, physically. They were diseased and neurotic, whereas he remained sane and calm, never quite willing to abandon his Victorian reticence and sense of morality to enter into a completely Bohemian existence. Such writers as Verlaine and Huysmans seemed drawn to the Church from an inner compulsion and need, while Machen never quite left it, except for a certain waywardness in the 1890's. Undoubtedly, the common root of Catholicism constitutes a basis for such comparisons; but the religiosity of the French Symbolists was vacillating and tortured, leading often to despair. They lived desperately and without restraint, while Machen's life was uneventful and above reproach. Only in *The Hill of Dreams* does he strike, on the surface at least, the common chords.

A few technical points of resemblance are in evidence despite the disparity in approach to similar subject matter. With Maeterlinck, Machen's literary connection is almost intangible because of the dissimilarity of their mediums; but Machen in his tales used an elliptical approach which hinted of events rather than expressing them directly—a peculiar mannerism reminiscent of Maeterlinck. The shadowy nature of the characters in both conveys the impression that one has been walking in the company of disembodied spirits, and events and actions are not readily discernible unless the reader is blessed with cryptic vision. Further, in *The Terror,* Machen conveyed the secret hostility of brute creation to humanity, a view also suggested by Maeterlinck.

With Baudelaire, Machen shared in common the dictum that the senses are but symbols of underlying truths: "The fancy that sensations are symbols and not realities hovered in his mind, and led him to speculate as to whether they could not actually be transmuted one into another." [55] Turquet-Milnes called Machen the most Baudelairian of contemporary writers because of his distrust of nature, his denunciation of *romans à clef,* his emphasis upon the importance of ecstasy, his withdrawal from common life, and his descriptive and sensory passages.[56] Several critics have linked Machen's name with those of Huysmans and Baudelaire; but Machen's own references suggest that he did not read the former at all until after the similarities had been harped upon; for the latter, he reserves only a complete silence.

In his own country, Machen knew both Wilde and Yeats; but it would be folly to assume any derivative influence on the basis of such casual acquaintanceships. Some similarities do exist, but the explanation undoubtedly lies in the breadth of the revolt against the conventional bourgeois approach to life, the typical Victorian attitude of the acceptance of surface realities. The works of Machen and Yeats are both imbued with the Celtic spirit which looks upon the material universe as a vast symbol. Both contain legend and myth of Celtic origin; but, where Yeats tends to concentrate on nationalism and the emancipation of Ireland, Machen converts the folklore into a hint of dark, primordial manifestations of evil still lurking in man. This pervasive influence of their native culture makes both Machen and Yeats appear to be foreign to *The Yellow Book* tradition, alien to the despair and cynicism of Dowson and Wilde, and to the preoccupation with sin and the sense of guilt and unworthiness.

Though Machen was not of the absinthe-sipping school, he took his gin, four-ale, and Australian burgundy on any occasion;

though not a catamite, he wore his cape; and though not a complete literary bounder, he saw some of his works between yellow covers. In short, he derived fringe benefits from the school without becoming a part of it. Where Wilde's *Picture of Dorian Gray* amalgamated particular sins into the embodiment of evil, Machen spoke only of transcendent sin and nameless infamies, of flaming eyes in a formless thing staring from a window, the symbol of all evil and hideous corruption.[57] And in an age when "Cynara" became a synonym for personal despair, Machen himself never despaired. His artist in *The Hill of Dreams* who succumbed to dissolution in the form of bottles darkly labeled and to a woman of ill repute was not an expression of individual depravity told from experience, but a universal symbol of a spirit too delicate to survive the banality of an unfavorable epoch of history.

Seen in historical perspective, it is evident that the symbolism and mysticism in Machen's works were neither derivative nor directly imitative. Evelyn Underhill's *Mysticism* provides a firm ground for understanding the origin of his mystical impulse and the relationship of symbolism to the expression of his beliefs. In fact, some passages in *Mysticism* are almost paraphrases or summaries from his works. The following excerpt not only partially defines the kind of experience Machen was interested in conveying, but also relates mysticism to love, to the literary impulse, and to religion: "He who falls in love with a woman and perceives—as the lover really does perceive—that the categorical term 'girl' veils a wondrous and unspeakable reality: he who, falling in love with nature, sees the light that never was on sea or land . . . he who falls in love with invisible things, or as we say 'undergoes conversion': all these have truly known for an instant something of the secret of the world." [58]

To the mystic, the symbol and the thing symbolized sometimes become fused so that he sees "visions" or hears "voices" "which we must look upon as the garment he has himself provided to veil that Reality upon which no man may look and live." [59] To communicate the perfect consummation, the mystic must rely upon symbolism and imagery and upon "rhythmic and exalted language which induces in sensitive persons something of the languid ecstasy of dream." [60] Although an immense variety of symbols are used, they fall into three patterns: first, the pilgrimage; second, mutual love or spiritual marriage; and third, transmutation. The most truthful symbol "will bring with it hints of mystery and wonder. . . . Its appeal will not be to the clever brain, but to the desirous heart, the intuitive sense, of man." [61]

In the pilgrimage category, one type is toward a definite goal, such as Jerusalem or the Beatific Vision, characterized by *The Divine Comedy*. The other "is the search for the 'Hidden Treasure which desires to be found,'" such as the quest of the Graal, which, "when regarded in its mystic aspect," is "an allegory of the adventures of the soul." [62] The second category, spiritual marriage, is best represented by the *Song of Songs*.[63] The third category, involving symbols of transmutation, is representative of divine immanence and is most typically expressed in the works of the spiritual alchemists, or hermetic philosophers, such as Boehme, Law, or Browne.[64]

Although the genuine mystic may belong to any theological order or to none, Christian symbolism is apparently more adaptable than that of other religions because it has produced more world renowned mystics, particularly among the Catholic saints.[65] The theory of emanations, which depends on a transcendent God, "*latens Deitas:* Who is therefore conceived as external to the world which He illuminates and vivifies," [66] and the theory of immanence, where God is present in all things, are united through Christ, the bridge between the finite and the infinite.[67] On the other hand, occultism sometimes breaks out in periods of mystical activity. Magic, like mysticism, is absorbed in transcendental matters, in the craving for hidden knowledge. Both magic rites and church ceremonies depend to a great extent on the psychical effect of ritual; but Evelyn Underhill quotes Patmore as saying, "'the work of the Church ends when the knowledge of God begins.'" [68]

The second part of *Mysticism* deals with the five stages of the mystic way: awakening or conversion, self-knowledge or purgation, illumination, surrender, and finally union, which is arrived at after successive stages of pleasure and pain.[69] This is much the same pattern, incidentally, that Machen led his main character through in *The Secret Glory* several years before the first edition of Evelyn Underhill's book appeared. In the first stage the conversion is generally abrupt, though sometimes gradual, resulting in an ineffable revelation: "The typical case is, of course, that of St. Paul: the sudden light, the voice, the ecstasy, the complete alteration of life." [70] In all cases the experience is incommunicable.[71]

Although only the practicing mystics know what the unitive life is, some of the quality exists in every artist, musician, scientist, in every individual who aspires to heroic endeavor, to beauty and truth and love and goodness, through the remaking of character around new and higher centers of life. The formula shown us by the mystics for achieving this perception of Reality is self-discipline, purging, new vision, and self-dedication. "This meaning, this secret plan of Creation, flames out, had we eyes to see, from every department of existence. Its exultant declarations come to us in all great music; its wild magic is the life of all romance." [72]

Evelyn Underhill's book serves very well to elucidate Machen's mystical credo, to point up the necessity for and purpose of his symbolism, and to link both to the literature of romance. In the works themselves, the key words which permeate the whole are "ineffable mystery"; and the understanding of their meaning constitutes the basis for divining Machen's artistic purpose. Since the senses do no more than hint at the true meaning of life, the evidence of the senses in the form of scientific treatise or realistic literature fails to reveal the significance of our being. "Mysteries can only be conveyed by symbols. . . ." [73] Machen uses fauns, satyrs, the great god Pan, the witches' Sabbath, and the Little People to symbolize the evil and diabolical forces in nature. He uses the Holy Graal to convey the common mythos of Plato's "fallen angels," the Biblical fall of man, and the conception of reincarnation—in other words, the sense of loss, of supernal knowledge once known and but vaguely remembered, and of the attainment of sanctity. Bacchus and the vine are symbols of divine intoxication or Plato's "divine madness." More in conformance with the extreme Idealism of Bishop Berkeley, Machen uses symbols to convey the idea of perichoresis or the interpenetration of one age with another and also the possibility of the alter ego.

Since the mystery is ineffable, the purpose of the symbol is, of course, not so much to rend the veil as to give some inkling that behind the veil is no dark void; not, in a sense, to reveal the mystery, but to intimate its presence.

To the initiated—in this case, those belonging to the cult of the mystic idealists—the meaning of the mystery is at once clear. All can take part in the rites who understand that life is more than it appears to be and who acknowledge the transcendence of the intuitive faculty. Machen ably summarizes his own position: "I chose the mysteries first and I chose them last: seeking always that secret which is hidden beneath the barley—to use the phrase of Eleusis—the one secret which is concealed beneath the various assemblage of sensible appearances." [74]

III *Weird and Occult*

The term "weird and occult" is better suited to describing Machen's works than "horror and supernatural" because, in the first place, Machen's works normally do not convey horror in the usual sense of physical fear and revulsion, but only in a spiritual sense of omnipresent sin and evil on a strictly transcendental plane. In the second place, many of his works have occult references without themselves falling into the category of either horror or supernatural.

Many of the occult works which Machen cataloged for Redway were medieval in origin. Whether Machen gave these texts more than a cursory glance in the course of his labors is difficult to determine. At least two persons thought that the influence was deep. Starrett said that Machen, with his "head full of curiously occult mediaevalism, privately acquired from yellowed palimpsests and dog-eared volumes of black letter, wrote a classic." [75] Lady Benson emphasized the same point in her description of Machen's aptness for the part of Bolingbroke the Conjuror in *Henry VI:* "I always feel about Arthur Machen that he is the only man I ever met who thoroughly understood the devil and when he was cast for this wizard part, knowing, as I did, how deeply in his earlier days he had studied the mysteries of the Black Art, as practiced in the Middle Ages, I felt that this casting was a singularly happy one." [76]

However, with the exception of Rabelais, who belonged more to the age of Humanism than to the Middle Ages, no heavy leanings on medieval works can be found in Machen's tales. Certainly the savor is there—an occasional allusion, Latin tags, the rites of the witches' Sabbath—but his attitude can best be brought into perspective by the confession that he found the Cabala of Casanova, which cost Madame d'Urfé so dearly, to be much more entertaining than the Cabala of Knorr von Rosenroth.[77] This tendency on Machen's part to treat very lightly or even to ridicule the foremost proponents of the occult sciences was quite in keeping with Rabelais, who devoted a section of his masterwork to the Queen of Whims, a dupe of the alchemists, Rosicrucians, and occult quacks. At any rate, though such names as Henry Cornelius Agrippa, Scott, Nostradamus, William Lilly, and Robertus de Fluctibus (Robert Fludd) appear from time to time, none of the allusions is detailed; nor does any one of them reveal a great familiarity with the author cited. Similarly, Machen's statements concerning Black Magic, alchemy, and witchcraft are general and fail to establish the source of his knowledge, which could just as well have been from a nineteenth-century study as from a medieval Faustbook. The Faustian element is nonetheless strong in his tales, and the growth of demonology was unquestionably medieval in origin.

A more definite source of inspiration for Machen was *The Arabian Nights*. Actually, with its fabulous adventure, its eroticism, and its occult and magical devices of jinns, genies, and magicians, *The Arabian Nights* represents a common oriental source for the adventurous, the erotic, and the Gothic elements of romance. Machen, however, did not adopt either the supernatural machinery or the atmosphere to create another *Vathek*. What he did try to convey was the quality of unbelievable magic by transmuting London into a Bagdad with Black Magicians, letters with the Rosicrucian seal, secret societies, strange meetings, and other odd things.[78]

By far the strongest element in his tales, the Celtic occult, was partially medieval in origin and partially from an earlier, darker period. Mage Merlin, the Faery Queen, the bell of Teilo Sant, and the fairy birds of Rhiannon frequently occur. The oral tradition, however, plays the largest role in his tales of terror and represents an environmental influence. Machen never converts the *Tylwyth Teg* into the benign fairies of the literary tradition followed by Shakespeare and Herrick. He always represents them as dwarfish, malignant creatures, practicing obscene and horrible rites, a conception which takes account of the feeling of fear inherent in such lore. In Professor John Rhŷs's study, *Celtic Folklore,* many of the facets of the oral tradition itemized can be found in Machen's works: the substitution of a fairy, usually dwarfish, wizened and malignant, for an infant in the cradle;[79] the story of the little girl who went away every day to play with the *Tylwyth Teg;*[80] the old woman who overheard an unintelligible language;[81] the conception of the soul as a pigmy or lizard;[82] "the belief in transformations or transmigrations";[83] the idea of the *Tylwyth Teg* as dwarfs;[84] the fact that fairies were once regarded as cannibals;[85] the theory that since fairies are associated with ancient sites, they may perhaps have been real people, such as the Picts, who lived in the Lowlands of Scotland, underground or in hillocks.[86] Machen claimed that this folklore was still a living thing; that, when he visited a town in Wales, the inhabitants still burned a light to keep out the Little People.[87] This statement proves that he acquired some of his knowledge of this body of lore through the oral tradition; but he could have gleaned some of the less popular embellishments from association with *Walford's Antiquarian.*

Also from the ancient past, Machen used material from Greek and Roman mythology, primarily suggested to him by the archeological discoveries in the Roman ruins near his childhood home. In this area, Machen was only interested in the darker side of the Pan legend.

Machen thought of most of his tales in the genre of the weird and occult as shilling shockers, but in the historical sense they do not quite fit into that category. Through Waite, a collector of "penny dreads," Machen could possibly have obtained some plots and ideas; but a compendium of works which he admitted having read belies the fact that he had any interest whatsoever in the pure Gothic novel. The original impetus was given to works of this type by the rapidly fading belief in supernatural agents during the Age of Reason: "When the Devil was dead, and God was good, and the fear of God a phrase, then the ghost story came into being to touch that old nerve that perceives, and fears, the supernatural." [88] The "shilling shocker," produced in answer to the new demand of lending libraries, was simply a thinly disguised compression or plagiarism of early Gothic novels, and this vogue stopped about 1820 with the surfeit of public appetite. In brevity, the shilling shockers formed a transition between the Gothic novels and the short tales of terror.[89] In 1817 the publication of *Frankenstein* introduced certain elements new to the Gothic novel; and by 1830, Scott's *Letters on Demonology and Witchcraft* certainly sounded the death knell of the devil and his allies: "The modern supernaturalism is more complex, more psychological than the terroristic, perhaps because nowadays man is more intellectual, his thought-processes more subtle." [90]

Machen's tales are older and at the same time more modern than the pure Gothic. He uses none of the machinery of the castle, the vaults, the hidden corridors, the innocent heroine, the inert hero, or the Byronic villain. He relies more upon psychological and psychical processes, upon dream supernaturalism, upon pseudoscientific devices. Yet, with all his modernity, his tales contain elements that are more ancient in origin than anything in the Gothic novel. Of the leading exponents of the Gothic, Machen is more on the side of Horace Walpole. Ann Radcliffe gives a rational and commonplace explanation of the horrible, but Machen leaves his supernatural forces surrounded in an aura of the inexplicable.

Aside from the purely Gothic writers, many of the prominent Romantics manifested an interest in the weird and occult. Balzac's "The Elixir of Life," Hawthorne's "The Birth Mark," Shelley's *Rosicrucian,* Byron's *Manfred,* Scott's *Letters on Demonology and Witchcraft,* Mrs. Shelley's *Frankenstein*—the idea for which came from Byron and Shelley—and a large portion of Poe's tales of terror and horror are but a few illustrations of this darker side of the Romantic nature. Machen's most obvious sources of inspiration are reflected in a parody of *The Great God Pan and the Inmost Light,* wherein a doctor pours fluids promiscuously together, letting chance produce the great experiment. The product smelled like "the decayed remains of Hawthorne and Edgar Allan Poe." [91] Machen's great affinity for these writers was self-admitted, and the parallel in the works lies in the emphasis on atmosphere by means of description rather than by creation of character or by conversation. All three writers make use of the devices of journals, diaries, or manuscripts to abet the illusion of the extraordinary. The strong similarity between Machen and Poe has been noted by numerous critics, and Machen has been variously classified above and below his predecessor in the power to thrill.

Moving closer toward Machen's own period, a reviewer for the *Westminster Gazette* asserted that Machen was the wildest imitator of the English school of Diabolists, modeled after the French.[92] That the element of diabolism, of infernal agencies and sacraments, of witches and the like, is strong in Machen's work is beyond dispute; but Stevenson, the only English contemporary whom Machen imitated, can scarcely be thought of either as a "school" or as a specialist in diabolism. Machen's name has frequently been linked with that of Le Fanu and Baudelaire, but the proof that he was even familiar with the works of these two authors is not decisive. Certainly, he shared with Baudelaire certain general traits in the use of symbolism and a common sense of the potency of sin; but Machen's works do not exude evil because, unlike Baudelaire, his hell was never personal.

In the 1890's, on the other hand, the forces at work which produced a genuine Romantic movement under the leadership of Stevenson and Kipling and which also produced the Symbolists and "art for art's sake" group were the same forces which enmeshed Machen at the crucial point of his career. Cornelius Weygandt made the observation that "The supernatural is not . . . necessary to romance" and is a lower and cruder form except with expert handling.[93] Demonology he termed "tainted romance."[94] Be that as it may, many of the prominent writers of the decade—Stevenson, Kipling, James, Wilde, Doyle, Yeats, and Wells—overlap into one or the other of these fields. Although Wells's *Time Machine* was published in 1895 after Machen's main ventures with weird stories were completed, a similarity exists in the notion of being able to transcend time. Wells, however, relied upon scientific machinery; Machen relied only upon the powers of imagination. Another parallel can be drawn between *The Island of Dr. Moreau* and *The Great God Pan* in the surgical experiments which revert men into beasts. Though the two writers were not dependent upon each other for ideas or techniques, Machen followed Wells's progress with considerable interest and commented early in 1946 that, in the absence of a book-selling revival, Wells had had to reinvent the devil.[95]

Doyle's peregrinations also fascinated Machen. Apparently a willing victim of the spiritualists, Doyle made occasional forays in his writings into mesmerism or long range Svengaliism; and, in 1926, he published a tome called *The History of Spiritualism*. Machen's main attraction to Doyle, however, was his superb creation of the mastersleuth, Sherlock Holmes. Dyson in *The Three Impostors* and in "The Inmost Light" is a similar character, though he does most of his sleuthing in the realm of paleontology in order to solve transcendental mysteries of fairy lore. Jordan-Smith calls Machen's one mystery story, *The Terror,* "far more exciting than the inventions of Conan Doyle." [96]

Machen's work is considerably like that of Henry James in the use of atmospheric tension to create the sense of nameless evil. Otherwise, no direct correlation exists between *The Turn of the Screw* and any of Machen's works. The same can be said of the relationship between Machen and Kipling. Machen mentions "The Miracle of Purun Bhagat" on more than one occasion, but none of his own tales of miraculous intervention bear any similarity. Machen does admit to having the general idea of Kipling's "ghostly Indian regiment" in his mind before he wrote "The Bowmen," but nothing more.[97]

The most marked influence from this period was derived from Stevenson. Weygandt classified *The Great God Pan* in a group belonging to a modern school of terror, owing something to *Dr. Jekyll and Mr. Hyde,* but harking back consciously to Maturin and Beckford.[98] The first influence mentioned, at any rate, is correct. Machen's notion of extracting the soul of man and leaving only the essence of evil through pseudoscientific means is very closely allied to the concept of man's dual nature expressed in *Dr. Jekyll and Mr. Hyde* and to the method used to bring about that schism.

Alongside the main literary movements of the later Victorian period ran a parallel interest in occult activities, which resulted in a spate of publications in the 1890's, some scientific and some otherwise, just as occurred in the correspondingly rebellious 1920's. In 1875, the Theosophical Society was founded by Helena Petrovna Blavatsky; in 1879, Christian Science, by Mary Baker Eddy; and in 1882, the Society for Psychical Research. Books appeared on spiritualism, magic, the kabalah, the Rosicrucians, phallicism, fairy lore, witches, and on the legend of the Holy Graal. Many prominent persons were at various times affiliated with one or the other of the occult movements; and Machen himself admitted, "I once belonged, by the way, to a Secret Order. . . ." [99] Among the books on occult subjects which Machen acknowledged having read in this period, besides Jennings' *Rosicrucians,* are Jennings' *Phallicism;* Waite's *Real History of the Rosicrucians, Doctrine and Literature of the Kabalah,* and *The Hidden Church of the Holy Graal;* Blavatsky's *Secret Doctrine;* Frazer's *The Golden Bough;* and Rhŷs's *The Arthurian Legend.* He probably also read Blavatsky's *Isis Unveiled;* Rhŷs's *Celtic Folk-lore* and *Lectures on the Origin and Growth of Religion as Illustrated by Celtic Heathendom;* and Waite's *Book of Black Magic.*

Despite his obvious interest, the evidence thus far compiled does not prove that Machen was an adept of the black arts or that he was even seriously involved with any of the groups or doctrines mentioned above. In fact, the evidence indicates that just as he was not a member of the Yeats, Wilde, Moore, or Irving circles, so also he was not a spiritualist, mesmerist, a practitioner of voodoo, or any other unorthodox science. His role seems to have been that of an observer from afar. Except for that of Stevenson, the influences from this period are coincidental and tenuous rather than actual.

The strongest link connecting Machen to present-day exponents of the weird and occult is the element of supernatural science, which Dorothy Scarborough describes as a distinctively modern development.[100] Just as weird science fiction anticipates many of the actual developments of science, so Machen anticipated lobotomy in the transcendental surgery of *The Great God Pan* and "The Inmost Light," and he professed to have anticipated wireless telegraphy also in the former of these works.[101] The most important junction between stories of the occult and supernatural and scientific fiction, according to J. O. Bailey, "lies in the story of some creature from a dimension beyond the third." [102] In this connection, Machen and Ray Bradbury are alike. Machen's theory of perichoresis or interpenetration of one age with another makes possible the survival of primordial beings, which are something other than three dimensional. For one adhering to such a philosophy as Machen's to relegate himself to the field of supernatural science is not so odd as it might seem because, as Bailey says, "Platonism and science seem, at first glance, strange companions, but the frontier regions of physics have looked for some years like mysticism." [103]

Machen's longevity made him a contemporary of every writer of weird and occult fiction since the publication of Stevenson's *Dr. Jekyll and Mr. Hyde.* Of the many prominent authors in this field who have earned some degree of distinction in the twentieth century—Bradbury, H. P. Lovecraft, Lord Dunsany, Blackwood, F. Marion Crawford, Montague Rhodes James, and Ambrose

Bierce—none could have had any great influence upon Machen except in his brief venture, 1914 to 1918, with purely supernatural fiction. And no such influences are in evidence. Of his atmospheric tales written in the 1890's, however, Edward Wagenknecht has said that no such terror exists in all literature as in *The House of Souls,* except perhaps in Lovecraft.[104] In other words, in this particular genre Machen was a strongly original writer who went beyond the literary tradition preceding him.

CHAPTER 4

Worked in Clay

WITH the biographical data, with Machen's outlook on life, and with the literary traditions which he followed well in mind, the critical evaluation of his works would be a relatively easy task were it not for their voluminousness and heterogeneity. Several of the main areas of his literary production have been tangentially covered in the preceding chapters. For example, his three autobiographical works—*Far Off Things, Things Near and Far,* and *The London Adventure*—were primary sources for facts of his life, for statements of philosophy, and for establishing literary influences, in conjunction, of course, with the introductions which he wrote for the Knopf editions of his work. These works are not stylistically without merit, but they are of little interest in revealing either the temper of the times through which he lived or significant details about the other literary figures with whom he was associated. In those respects, his personal letters are of greater interest.

Machen's *juvenilia* and minor works which have not been extensively republished have already been analyzed in an attempt to establish his literary direction and the nature of his talent. The very large body of his expository essays have been examined to gain some insight into his basic beliefs concerning major spheres of human endeavor. Although the ideas expressed in these writings are essentially sincere and consistent with other sources, the general tone of the essays is dogmatic and calculated to excite controversy. They represent, therefore, a rather high order of journalism, but a rather dubious form of art. What now remains is to consider some of his major works in relation to the literary traditions established in the last chapter. Even here, the selection will have to be limited and arbitrary because his tales of the weird and occult are by themselves voluminous.

I *Armchair Essays*

In 1899 Machen dashed off *Hieroglyphics,* the only book he ever wrote without enduring cruel pain.[1] In it he is primarily concerned with making the distinction between fine and ordinary literature. The development is professedly a peculiar cyclical mode of discoursing from the mouth of an obscure literary hermit, an avowed mystic, who, like Coleridge, believed himself to have an esoteric philosophy or "system" for acquiring the ultimate truths about literature.[2] Basically, *Hieroglyphics* is impressionistic criticism of the type made popular during the Romantic period.

Machen's position on the staff of *Literature* had forced him for the first time to give serious consideration to the importance of critical standards, and *Hieroglyphics* was the culmination of his logical processes as applied to embryonic themes expressed in that periodical. Only one essay "Unconscious Magic" was preserved almost intact in the larger work. This essay is an expression of the idea that great artists are seldom conscious of what they are actually producing. Machen cited several examples of authors who were challenging current customs and ways of life, but who have survived despite allusions to their own era. Thus, Tennyson's *Idylls of the King* dealt with liberal institutions; Cervantes intended to reform current perversity in literary taste; Rabelais expressed hatred of clericalism; Sterne was laughing at local enemies; Dickens was exposing bribery and corruption; and Shelley was as much concerned with the political as the poetical. Yet Machen maintained that, despite the author's intent, the real meaning of Cervantes is the quintessence of all the marvel and wonder and awe of chivalry; of Rabelais, the eternal mystic mirth like a spring of fresh life; and of *Pickwick,* the romance of the picaro. From this seeming paradox, Machen concluded: "Literature is full of secrets, but perhaps it offers no stranger matter for our consideration than melodies unheard by those who made them, than Siren songs that never came to Siren's ears." [3]

As the basic tenet of *Hieroglyphics,* Machen maintains that fine literature is distinguished by the quality of ecstasy.[4] "Substitute, if you like, rapture, beauty, adoration, wonder, awe, mystery, sense of the unknown, desire for the unknown . . ."—all of which convey a sense of "withdrawal from the common life and the common consciousness. . . ." [5] By way of example, he then analyzes many works which possess the quality of which he speaks. To distinguish between art and artifice, he classifies *The Pickwick Papers* as art and *Vanity Fair* as artifice.[6] Within each of the two divisions he further segregates by stating that *Vanity Fair* ranks among the best of plain literature[7] and the *Odyssey* toward the topmost rank in fine art.[8] For the *roman à clef,* which he thinks of simply as a real story with substituted names, he has the greatest contempt[9] and would classify it as the very meanest attempt at artifice.

The text of *Hieroglyphics* evolves from four major works: the *Odyssey, Pickwick, Don Quixote,* and *Gargantua.* Each has its own symbol. The *Odyssey* is read because we are supernatural creatures. It contains "echoes of the eternal song . . ." and "symbolizes . . . amazing and beautiful things. . . ." [10] *Don Quixote* reveals an "eternal moral . . . the strife . . . between ecstasy and the common life . . ." which is the "tragedy of life itself, symbolized." [11] In Rabelais, the ecstasy or withdrawal from common life is expressed through obscenity and the symbol of the vine.[12] In a lesser sense, *Pickwick* also utilizes the Bacchic cultus as a symbol of ecstasy.[13] All of these interpretations may seem illogical; but Machen asserts that art is mystical in its implications, not logical.[14]

From the definition of terms and the limitation of extremes, Machen proceeds to define what art is by stating what it is not. In the first place, he claims that fidelity to life is not a criterion because, if it were, the *Morte d'Arthur* and "Kubla Khan" would be eliminated.[15] In the second place, mere plotting or clever choice of incident is not a criterion because every newspaper reporter must possess that talent in greater or lesser degree; and it is generally agreed that the daily newspaper is not the place to look for literary masterpieces.[16] In the third place, utilitarian style is not a criterion since every commercial clerk must have such ability.[17]

From that point Machen proceeds to a consideration of many novels on the basis of the foregoing principles. He places the works of Thackeray, Jane Austen, Trollope, and "poor, dreary, draggle-tailed George Eliot" in the category of plain literature.[18] In other words, in Machen's consideration of these works, there is no art involved, merely a matter of taste.[19] For example, *Madame Bovary* and *Jackie's Holiday* are of the same genus though specifically differentiated.[20]

By the standards of rationalism or materialism, "Keats would be a queer kind of madman," and "the story of the Graal lunacy"; and by spiritual or mystic standards, "*Pride and Prejudice* is not fine literature, and the works of George Eliot are the works of a superior insect. . . ." [21] The crux, therefore, of the critical standards of *Hieroglyphics* obviously lies in making a choice between two schismatic solutions to life.

In his discursive way, Machen then proceeds to an analysis of *Don Quixote* in terms of the four principles of the genesis of art: the idea or conception, plot, construction, and style. His contention is that perfection in art is perfection in all four of these elements, but that only the idea or conception is pure art and that the plot and construction are the most mechanical and least significant elements. Thus, *Dr. Jekyll and Mr. Hyde* barely falls into the category of art because of its idea, though Machen felt the manner of execution to be questionably artistic;[22] *Two on a Tower* by Hardy belongs in the same group by virtue of the fact that it is "a symbol of Love, of an ecstasy . . .";[23] Poe's Dupin is also in the class of fine art;[24] and lyric poetry, which is almost pure idea, is the purest form of art. *Don Quixote* ranks very high as an expression of the essential quality of ecstasy. It is "the eternal quest of the unknown." Cervantes' commentary on contemporary affairs is the weakest element of the book because, as Machen maintains in accordance with the dictum of Poe, allegory is a literary vice. In order to read *Pilgrim's Progress* with enjoyment, for example, one must forget "that the allegory exists." To summarize his position, he considers that despite the wretched plan and the clumsy construction of *Lycidas,* it is also perfect beauty:[25] "It is the very soul set to music; its austere and exquisite rapture thrills one so that I could almost say: He who understands the mystery and beauty of *Lycidas* understands also the final and eternal secret of art and life and man." [26]

The next section of *Hieroglyphics* is concerned with the comparison between *The Pickwick Papers* and *Pantagruel.* Although Machen considers Rabelais to be less readable and his plan more obscure, he deems his work to represent a greater achievement in terms of the principle of ecstasy because it is further removed from the daily round.[27]

Certainly the works of Rabelais, Hardy, Dickens, and Cervantes all have some social value and intent. But art so far transcends the purpose of the author that it is questionable whether artists really understand the true value of their work at the moment of writing.[28] "Art is always miraculous. In its origin, in its working, in its results it is beyond and above explanation, and the artist's unconsciousness is only one phase of its infinite mysteries." [29] Returning to his thesis, Machen emphasizes more strongly that rationalism has nothing to do with art and that the position of the rationalist is wholly wrong.[30] Reason is useful in the affairs of common, everyday existence; but when applied to art, it fails to reveal any of the greater underlying truths. "For Artifice is of Time, but Art is of Eternity." [31]

Next, Machen asserts that Poe was wrong in distinguishing beauty and truth and further in error by insisting that poetry alone should be beautiful. Chanting and incantation, Machen claims, are natural to man as witnessed by ceremonies of savage tribes and religious ritual of civilized peoples. Furthermore, he states that animals possess artifice, but art and ecstasy are natural only to man. He considers two American novels in the light of his principles—*Huckleberry Finn* and Mary E. Wilkins Freeman's *Pembroke*—and finds that, at least in part, they both qualify as art according to his standards.

Finally, Machen itemizes some of the devices which the authors whom he has considered used to make their work deliberately unreal. Rabelais professed to use a manuscript found in a tomb; Cervantes, an Arabic manuscript; and Hawthorne, documents found in the customhouse. Historical novels utilize the device of remoteness in time and remoteness in space.[32] Some writers rely upon poetic diction. The genius of the artist, in itself inexplicable, is manifested through a fine style which carries "suggestion beyond the bourne of thought. . . ." Such a style may be "the veil and visible body of concealed mysteries," but it "is always plain on the surface." [33] The secret of making literature is incommunicable, and even artifice cannot always be taught. "Art is a miracle, superior to the laws." [34]

The criticisms of *Hieroglyphics* when it first appeared were, generally speaking, half laudatory and half derogatory; but Machen never forgave Quiller-Couch for his high-handed, unfavorable comments.[35] Other unfavorable criticism was embodied in such words and phrases as "unclear," "unwholesome," "effeminate," "lacking in catholicity of taste," "one-sided," and "without profundity." [36] The same critics, however, found the work partly true, very readable, clever, piquant, brilliantly written, bubbling over with pugnacities, and containing some shrewd analysis.[37] "He talks (like the Walrus) of many things, of office boys, of Coleridge, of words that end in 'ings'; of Homer and of Dickens, of literature, of art; of books that bore and 'lonely' books, which have a 'soul apart.'" [38]

The critics of the 1920's, on the other hand, had nothing but praise. Even C. Lewis Hind grudgingly admitted that *Hieroglyphics* could make him a Machenite if anything could.[39] The reviewer for *The Times Literary Supplement* commented on the great challenge of the book,[40] and August Derleth proclaimed it a body of remarkably brilliant exposition which richly deserves to be far more widely read than it has been.[41] Concerning the type of criticism which *Hieroglyphics* exemplifies, R. Ellis Roberts commented: "His theory has been adopted, or very likely rediscovered, by that school of critics who insist that great art is appreciated, is apprehended immediately; there is an act of faith towards art, as towards religion, and an art which does not, in some way, reach the eternal, is little better than *décor,* a background, lovely and delicate no doubt, but irrelevant as a dinner-engagement on the Day of Judgment." [42]

For the first time in his career, Machen had abandoned the imitative or pseudoartistic style. It is fairly easy to infer which of the many styles he had assumed was the one uniquely his. If ease of reading and ease of writing are criteria, the quality of this book is most distinctively his own. No longer are heard the echoes of Rabelais, Burton, Stevenson, or Pater; and, though a slight note of Coleridge or Lamb may have entered in, the cyclical discourse and the whimsy are tempered by the inexorable logic of Machen.

The test of a work of criticism lies not so much in its manner of presentation as in its ability to give to the reader new insight into works of art, either by presenting hitherto unknown facts, by lighting up obscure passages, or by superimposing an interpretation rendered in terms of a different philosophy. By these standards Henry Savage has ably captured the essence of *Hieroglyphics* by saying that the work invites "continual analysis until it is either accepted or refuted," that it is the only English work which adequately explains Rabelais, and that it allows Machen a permanent place in literature.[43]

When applied to his own creative works, the standards of *Hieroglyphics* represent, to a great extent, simply a rationalization of what Machen had been trying to accomplish in the field of art. In the many varied modes and manners of expression, he had been quite evidently obsessed with a singleness of purpose—to convey the feeling of awe and wonder, to unveil the secret meaning beneath the commonest things. That he was consistent in this belief is shown by his attempt in later life to instill some of its meaning into an early work, *The Anatomy of Tobacco.* In 1926, he maintained that just as Rabelais had made a great song of joy and triumph of unsavory matters, or just as Cervantes made a madman's misadventures into a great romance and as Dickens had converted cockneydom, so he himself had "endeavoured to shew that there are wonders, secrets, mysteries, rarities, delights, even in an ounce of shag tobacco and a clay pipe." [44] Like Poe's "Rationale of Verse," Machen's *Hieroglyphics* represents a crystallization of his artistic standards.

On the favorable side, *Hieroglyphics* is a powerfully challenging and provocative work. In this age of Materialism, of realistic and naturalistic writing, of negative denouements, of careless style, it gives the reader a refreshing view of Idealism, of limitless worlds beyond his own, of a positive glory, and of pure incantation and magic in the written word. It is a return to absolute standards in this world of relative values. The best use *Hieroglyphics* could be put to would be to place it in a modern curriculum for all aspiring artists and critics to read. In the 1920's it was used as a text at Cornell University, but the temper of the 1960's has so altered that even the remote possibility of the rightness of opposing views is now often discountenanced. At any rate, no other work of Romantic criticism has quite the scope or the persuasiveness of *Hieroglyphics.*

To state unequivocally that it is a classic, however, would be somewhat hyperbolic. It is no Aphrodite rising unblemished from the sea, complete and self-contained in its own fulfillment. A few loose strands of hair, a mutilated finger or two, and a few distortions here and there mar its perfection. For one thing, the book leaves something to be desired in the lack of consideration of more than a few of the most prominent works. For another, the very fine distinction between high artifice and art appears somewhat arbitrary—the difference between Swift and Rabelais, for example. Machen's position is clear, however: the proper study of mankind is not man. Art must possess something more. That Machen was aware of the shortcomings of his critical study can be seen in his numerous later elaborations of embryonic themes in *Hieroglyphics*. That he was not totally free of prejudice may be seen in his diatribes against Tolstoi, whom he had never read because he believed him to be a naturalist, and against Joyce, whom he had read only slightly and whose style he believed to be deliberate obfuscation. In the final analysis, *Hieroglyphics* is a purist doctrine applied to literature to distinguish the great from the small, and "if a book have nothing in it of the old incantation of the forest and the mountain—then it is nothing." [45]

Over a score of years later, Machen wrote another work completely in the Romantic tradition in which he used the same cyclical logic as in *Hieroglyphics.* This series of personal essays called *Dog and Duck* had been originally published in *The Lyons Mail.* His servitude to *The Evening News* had gentled him; and he emerged once more to the world without anger, without dogmatism, without bitterness. Dog and Duck, he insisted, was a slightly antiquated game, dating back at least to the days of Charles II. Actually, Machen invented the game himself. The mood of the whole book is set by the obsolescent quality of its title piece, by the eccentric individuality of the author, and by the pervading love of old customs and traditions. Generally speaking, the essays are concerned with ancient customs, superstitions, and human foibles. The style, somewhat altered from that of his earlier days through the influence of journalism, is more simple and direct but it does not sacrifice the suggestion of seventeenth-century archaism that enhances its quaintness and charm.

"Why New Year," "On Valentines and Other Things," "On Simnel-cakes," "'April Fool,'" "The Merry Month of May," and "A Midsummer Night's Dream"—all dredge back into the folk heritage of the race to explain in an entertaining way the origin of some of the oddest human rites and customs, usually with a bit of Machenesque philosophy lightly stated as a parting word of wisdom. For example, he ends "On Valentines and Other Things" by saying, "Thus, ancient ribaldry outlasts grave science." [46] In "'April Fool'" he considers, somewhat nostalgically, the dying custom whereby novices were sent to fetch pigeon's milk and strapfoil and to borrow an "ibid." From that observation he digresses to a comment about human nature: people will believe anything. Then, borrowing a bit of philosophy from Aristotle, he conjectures that such foolery probably originated in order to purge madness and folly by a day of excess. Finally he adds his own touch when he concludes that others say it is an ancient rite illustrating the craziness of most of the business of the world.[47]

"The Merry Month of May" considers with regret that the laughter and merriment surrounding Morris dances and the Maypole are done for. Now the world has Bolshevist anthems. Humor is close to sadness, the "exquisite by-product of a world which is seen to be all wrong. . . ."[48] "A Midsummer Night's Dream" is concerned with the fairies of Shakespeare, Herrick, and Hans Christian Andersen. The opening paragraphs, however, are merely a lead to ramble on about his own theories about fairies. " 'A Thorough Change' " deals with the subject of vacationing. The London people go to Brighton because it is an imitation of London. The people who change to remain the same are right.[49] Two titles most suggestive of *Essays of Elia* are "Roast Goose" and "Where Are the Fogs of Yesteryears?"; and the same emphasis upon the comforts of food and drink is present. In the first, however, Machen skips lightly over the goose to the thyme stuffing and from thence to "thymol," a powerful disinfectant, in order to express his theory of "traditional wisdom in meat, drink, and medicine." Old women rubbed seaweed, which is strong in iodine, on goiters, performing by intuition what medical science had not yet discovered.[50]

In almost every essay can be found a Machenism, either a pet theory or a satirical reference to some institution or idea against which he waged continual war. In "Martinmas" he claims that the Puritans hated bearbaiting not because of the pain to the bear but because of the pleasure to the spectator;[51] in "A Talk for Twelfth Night" he takes a customary tilt at Baconians; in "Some February Stars" he ridicules astrology; and in "March and a Moral" he deplores the mechanical crafts as heartily as William Morris did.

The pattern of the essays is always the same. He starts off with some catchy paradox or striking misrepresentation of fact which he then proceeds to refute in the same roundabout manner that he used in *Hieroglyphics*. For example, he begins "The Poor Victorians" with the customary prim and proper tea parties, attributing to the age its usual characteristics of decorum and reticence. Then he cites Tennyson's "Maud," Rossetti's "Jenny," Swinburne's *Poems and Ballads,* and Dickens' *The Welcome Guest* to show that the Victorian period was actually characterized by jollity and liberty, by rare vintages and fine cigars. Having presented a picture of cheer and comfort, he proceeds to contrast it with the night clubs of the 1920's where whiskey is served in coffee cups and flappers get "snow." And the art of Tennyson, Rossetti, Swinburne, Dickens, Thackeray, and the Pre-Raphaelites he contrasts with the modern art of Cubism, Vorticism, Post-Impressionism, free verse, and naturalistic novels. The title of the essay is indicative of the whimsical irony with which the subject is treated.[52]

Although Machen repeated phrases, sentences, and ideas constantly throughout his works, in no other work than *Dog and Duck* are they more charmingly and cleverly stated or more in harmony with the medium in which they are expressed. *The Secret Glory* seems charged with rancor and bias. In "St. George and the Dragon," on the other hand, when he defines school as "the place where ignorance of everything that matters is so carefully imparted,"[53] the statement is quite in keeping with the humorous quality of the essay, the purpose of which is to entertain rather than to harangue. Another parallel of the same kind can be drawn from *The Hill of Dreams* where he places ridicule of materialism and science in a purely spiritual environment; but in the essay "Stuff—and Science" he proceeds from the mathematical contradiction of Achilles and the tortoise to the conclusion that abstract and absolute science is nonsense; and his message is "*Do not let the doctor interfere with your dinner.*"[54] Also in "How to Spend Christmas," his ironical condemnation of modern materialism is in harmony with the whimsical logic: "the more comfortable we become, the less we know of comfort." In other words, the best place to spend our holiday, if modernists are right, would be in jail where the environment is scientifically controlled.[55]

With his description of the game Dog and Duck, two reviewers suspected Machen of pulling the reader's leg. One of them remembered too clearly Machen's admission of the fictitious character of "The Bowmen."[56] A. S. Godwin, a correspondent to *The Times Literary Supplement,* affirmed the authenticity of the game: "Let me assure you that the game is a very real one. . . ."[57]

Lady Benson also confirmed the existence of the game in a few phrases: "Delighting in simple pleasures, a game of bowls or 'Dog and Duck' with a tankard of ale and a huge pipe. . . ." [58] Actually, Machen was less concerned with the athletic version—an odd bowling game which he created to play in his own backyard—than he was with its namesake, also an invention of his: a private concoction which was the forerunner of the dry martini, made with gin and sauterne in equal parts and too much bitters.

As usual with most of Machen's works, *Dog and Duck* received both favorable and adverse criticism. The worst charge leveled against it was the journalistic nature of the essays. To be sure, when they are studied in relation to their own time, this challenge to their literary quality has an undisputed basis in fact. The book *Modern Grub Street and Other Essays* shows a remarkable similarity between the careers of A. St. John Adcock and Machen. Adcock contributed to many of the same magazines and evening papers, and he had done his turnovers for *The Globe*.[59] The essays in *Modern Grub Street* contain many reminiscences of old London and deplore the traffic, the hubbub and general furor of the present.[60] Adcock also deplores the passing of the old inns: "Soon there will be nobody who can rightly remember Old Serjeants' Inn and the broad archway that opened into it out of Chancery Lane. . . ." [61] As far as selection of material was concerned, Machen evidently followed the pattern of other commercial writers of the day. He acquired his knowledge of many of these subjects, however, as early as 1887 when he wrote filler articles for *Walford's Antiquarian*.

Of the favorable reviewers, even those who were not completely in accord about the merits of the book had some word of commendation for the style in which it was written. Also, most of them agreed that it had a certain degree of wit and charm. The reviewer for the *New York Times Book Review and Magazine* wrote the most laudatory critique of all. He itemized the essential elements of a personal essay—absolute casuality, seeming spontaneity, wisdom, and mellow wit—and claimed that Machen satisfied all requisites in his entertaining and enlivening book, "shot with shafts of wit, stuffed with matured advice. . . ." Of these essays, reminiscent of Dickens and Lamb, written in the older and higher literary sense, he further maintained, "it is clear that most of the papers are new, and that such as may embody earlier material have been elaborated and rewritten." He concluded that they would have the reader recapture the relish for life and that they are literature in the highest sense.[62]

In one way, the personal essay was Machen's forte. He expressed himself with ease and grace and lucidity. Such was his natural style, the one he used in correspondence. Thus, despite the obvious formulized pattern, *Dog and Duck* is almost as delightful a work as one can find in this field. What ranks Machen below the very great is that he could not appear disarmingly simple or seemingly artless. His intellectuality and his logic show through. He relies too much on exposition and not enough on the powers of the imagination. Furthermore, his personality was too complex to be fully expressible in terms of a single medium. His mystical and spiritual nature found other outlets.

II *The Rose of Fire*

Although Machen wrote few works which can be called systematic symbolism or comprehensive mysticism, he seldom wrote anything in which he did not insert some symbol or mystical overtone. Also, though the symbols vary from work to work, certain ones became his favorite means of expression. For example, as early as *The Chronicle of Clemendy,* he had already hit upon golden bells, everlasting music, the rose, the flame, and faintly remembered dreams. These symbols became the machinery for achieving mystical communion and sanctity. On the other hand, in his weird and occult tales, he used a standard set of symbols, already discussed, to represent the coeval state of evil, sorcery, demonology, and infamy. Although mysticism in the usual sense denotes visions of a sanctified nature, Machen celebrated many of the mysteries of the pre-Christian era which were held in worship of the darker deities; and when Machen stated that every branch of human knowledge vanishes into mystery,[63] he was not segregating the infernal from the supernal.

When, in 1895, Machen began *The Hill of Dreams,* his symbols were already well formulated; but he had yet to merge them into a work of serious artistic import. This experimental novel, almost esoterically preoccupied with symbols and the inner life, was an effort to convey the workings of the soul. As in James Joyce's *Ulysses,* a thin skein of incident can be traced. Lucian Taylor, son of a clergyman with a small living, resides near the ruins of an old

Roman fort. His education is interrupted when his father's income diminishes; and he adopts a literary career, drifting closer and closer to nature and farther and farther from reality. The crisis of his adolescence brings forth the awakening of physical desire, and at the same time makes him a mortal enemy of hypocrisy and convention. In young manhood he learns of love from Annie Morgan, but by this time he is so withdrawn within himself that he dwells only on the psychological sensation rather than on physical fulfillment. Instead of adopting normal means of the expression of passion, he scourges himself like an ascetic and limns books in honor of his beloved. On the receipt of a legacy, he removes to London where he falls deeper and deeper under the spell of evil. Amidst sordid surroundings, addicted to drugs, and married to a prostitute, he dwells more and more frequently on the beauty of his former life. Like Marcel Proust's *A la Recherche du Temps Perdu,* in recurrent symphonic measure, sensation recalls past moments; and the love for Annie, who married another, is rather the love of love itself. The gradual decay of the spirit and the disintegration of the soul finally end in suicide.

H. S. Darlington felt that the book was meant to show sex as the basis of religion; and in a letter to Parsons dated July 11, 1924, he presented two elaborate, parallel interpretations, one religious and the other Freudian. Machen's primary concern, however, was neither with sex nor religion, but with the struggle of the artist against the crass materialism and commercialism which deprived him of his integrity and his right to create according to his own inclinations. Although the main symbols were undeniably sexual in connotation, sex in itself was not important to Machen. Of Casanova, he wrote: "the more openly he reveals, the more deeply he conceals the mysteries. For the fact is that all the real secrets are ineffable; the secrets of the wood; the secrets of the flower and the secrets of the flame; and the secrets of the Faith." [64] The symbol, for Machen, had no meaning in itself; it only served as a clue to the thing signified:

> It was possible, he thought, that a whole continent of knowledge had been undiscovered; the energies of man having been expended in unimportant and foolish directions. Modern ingenuity had been employed on such trifles as locomotive engines, electric cables, and cantilever bridges; on elaborate devices for bringing uninteresting people

nearer together; the ancients had been almost as foolish, because they had mistaken the symbol for the thing signified. It was not the material banquet which really mattered, but the thought of it; it was almost as futile to eat and take emetics and eat again as to invent telephones and high-pressure boilers.[65]

Although Darlington's interpretation is an obvious rationalization, it is indicative of the suggestiveness and fluidity of the symbols.

The events of Machen's early life and the expository and satirical passages in *The Hill of Dreams* show quite clearly that the symbolism refers to the soul of the artist in his struggle for creativity. In this light, Lucian's dream of the faun on the fairy hill, his feelings of mad panic terror, of ecstasy and shame signify the awakening of the creative impulse.[66] His comparatively casual experiences with Annie become the basis of an idealization of all women,[67] an image of beauty for which he scourges himself and renounces the world; and he creates in his own fancy the garden of Avallaunius, representing artistic fulfillment. But in London, Lucian's literary endeavors become the symbol of desolation,[68] the gray street a symbol of his chill and dreary life.[69] And the woman with bronze hair and the argent gleam in her eyes is the prostitution of art to commercial standards[70] which can only end in figurative death to the artist.

The same symbols previously used in other works are here repeated, except that they are less sensational. The dream of the faun and the feeling of panic terror suggest the reappearance of the great god Pan;[71] the reference to Roman ruins takes the form of a fanciful reconstruction of an entire villa, around which embryonic idea the whole book is designed and to which the original title *The Garden of Avallaunius* refers; the atavistic symbol of the Little People is suggested in a scene where some small boys torture a pup;[72] and the street scene, not unlike a witches' Sabbath, symbolizes the evil and corruption besetting the soul of the artist.[73]

From one approach, the novel presents a detailed examination of the inner changes wrought by adolescence, with death—that is, spiritual death—resulting from the realization of the necessity to compromise. But, from a larger point of view, the symbolism conveys the perennial conflict of the sensitive person against a world without spiritual values. At any rate, the impact is not psychological. As in *Pelleas and Melisande,* the characters are shadowy enough and the symbols sufficiently elusive so as to delineate in the manner of a silhouette that indefinable essence of the corporeal self, the soul. The novel is completely original in its conception and belongs to no established pattern. As an experimental work, it may have been an incentive to later fantastic and symbolic books.[74] Joyce and Virginia Woolf, considerably more Freudian and psychological than Machen, nonetheless display the same marked individuality with respect to style; and the symphonic interludes of recollection of times past in Proust are not far afield from Machen's reiteration of the symbol of the Beloved in everything.[75]

Although Hillyer asserted that *The Hill of Dreams* is Machen's masterpiece of mysticism,[76] the work is basically symbolistic. A few random allusions here and there suggest the approach to mysticism—the flame in Lucian's dream of the fort,[77] the hint of mysteries,[78] the usual mystic esses,[79] and a mention of *Lumen de Lumine,* an alchemical treatise by Thomas Vaughan;[80] but only in the purely descriptive passages of nature is there any rapport or communion, the attempt to express the inexpressible through the creation of mood.[81] In the more occult sense of being initiated into the secret rites of the worshipers of beauty, however, a kind of purity and sanctification emerges through Lucian's flagellation and asceticism until a fragmentary glimpse of the ineffable mystery is produced—the "longing for longing, the love of love . . ." which is not love of woman "but the desire of womanhood, the Eros of the unknown. . . ." [82]

Though the mystical elements appear on the surface to be slight, many critics noted that the quality nevertheless exists; and Machen himself explained it as due to the curious incantation of the countryside—*aliquid latet*—where suddenly in a commonplace field the land would fall away and one would look down through a dark wood of ancient thorn trees to the reeds of a marsh.[83] Machen once saw on an altar the words, " 'The unseen is here and calleth to thee' "; and this sentence suggested to him that mysticism is simply extended sacramentalism.[84] Hillyer observed that to Machen facts were merely the symbols of the great sacrament;[85] and Cuthbert Wright reiterated the same idea when he commented that Machen's "reaction to landscape is, essentially, the platonic and sacramental view of nature . . ." where appearances are the veil and the fleshly symbols of divine realities.[86]

Appropriate as these evaluations may be when applied to Machen's works as a whole, the point seems only secondary in respect to *The Hill of Dreams.* Until after the turn of the century, his works were singularly devoid of any religious references, even in an unorthodox sense. Even though Machen was always a consistent exponent of mystery,[87] that trait alone does not necessarily constitute true Mysticism; and the literary product of such a philosophy might equally well be termed Romanticism, Symbolism, or fantasy. Machen had a tendency in later life to apply all of his ideas retroactively to earlier days, and many commentators were thereby misled into exaggerating incipient and embryonic manifestations. In this sense, then, of a premonitory characteristic, not predominant in *The Hill of Dreams* itself, Hillyer's statement of Machen's search for spiritual values has greater validity:

> Under such circumstances the world about him becomes merely a collection of keys, beautifully wrought by "the art-magic of God," which in the hands of the mystic, unlock the doors to that world beyond the world, that dwelling house of the ineffable Mystery whose rays, penetrating the material world, give even the darkest sinner his moments of holiness and the commonest mortal his hint of vision.[88]

Hillyer comes closer to the truth when he uses the term "Christian mysticism": a combination of the ecstasy of inner beauty and of the robust, sunlight joy of the Greeks.[89] At least the element of renunciation to achieve spiritual beauty is strong, and so is the element of pagan symbolism. Hillyer further maintains that *The Hill of Dreams* is an epic of the spiritual battle between the beautiful which builds walls of the celestial city in the mind of man and the unutterable evil which makes war against that beauty.[90] The work is certainly concerned with beauty and evil; but if the reader chooses to see a new Jerusalem in a pagan garden of delights, as the Holy Church may be construed from the *Song of Solomon,* then the virtue lies in the symbolism and not in the mystical qualities. This "Gorgeous, magnificent symbolism that is at once satire and tragedy"[91] is the means by which Machen transmutes ugliness to beauty, reveals the torment of an anguished soul in its awakening and in its destruction, and conveys the shadowy essences beneath the external realities.

One review, possibly written by Lord Alfred Douglas, deserves special attention because it captures so uniquely the rarity of some of Machen's best passages:

> There is something sinister in the beauty of Mr. Machen's book. It is like some strangely shaped orchid, the color of which is fierce and terrible, and its perfume is haunting to suffocation by reason of its intolerable sweetness. The cruelty of the book is more savage than any of the cruelty which the book describes. . . .
>
> For in *The Hill of Dreams* you seem to be shown a lovely sensitive boy who has fashioned himself a white palace of beauty in his own mind. He has time only to realize its full beauty when disease lays its cold touch upon him, and gathers him into her grip until he lies decaying and horrible, seeing his own decay and seeing that his decay makes the white palace foul.
>
> . . . and his prose has the rhythmic beat of some dreadful Oriental instrument, insistent, monotonous, haunting; and still the soft tone of one careful flute sounds on, and keeps the nerves alive to the slow and growing pain of the rhythmic beat. . . .
>
> It is like some dreadful liturgy of self-inflicted pain, set to measured music: and the cadence of that music becomes intolerable by its suave phrasing and perfect modulation. The last long chapter with its recurring themes is a masterpiece of prose, and in its way unique.[92]

Somewhat unwittingly, Machen created in *The Hill of Dreams* both a monument and an epitaph for the Aesthetic-Decadent period. The de-emphasis of form and plot and the emphasis upon sensation and symbol are eminently characteristic of the age. The theme embodies cruelty and perversity; the style embodies aestheticism. When placed in juxtaposition, the two become mutually destructive forces, ending in decay and dissolution. Oddly enough, that is the way the age ended. Theories of beauty ended in the corruption of diseased lives. Madeleine Cazamian has called *The Hill of Dreams* "without doubt the most decadent book in all of English literature." [93] Machen, like Thomas Mann in *The Magic Mountain,* held up the mirror to an epoch.

In 1897, upon the completion of the work just considered, Machen began to expand his more purely mystical manner in a series of short sketches called *Ornaments in Jade*. "Holy Things," "Midsummer," and "Nature" are all rather unsuccessful attempts to convey ecstatic union through his usual series of symbols: music, incense, the bell, ritual, and burning pools at sunset. In "Nature" the splendor of fire was "as if all precious things were cast into its furnace pools, as if gold and roses and jewels became flame." He was trying to tell the story of " 'a wonderful and incredible passion.' " [94]

Only one of these sketches, "The Rose Garden," embodies, however, all of the elements necessary to a true piece of mysticism. Like petals unfolding, the soul of a woman embraces the deep rest of the night, veiled with half-light and half-shadow, and achieves rapport with the shapes, sounds, and sights around her. She is as ecstatic as a poet dreaming under roses, having neither reality nor substance: "He had always told her that there was only one existence, one science, one religion, that the external world was but a variegated shadow, which might either conceal or reveal the truth. . . . He had shewn her that bodily rapture might be the ritual and expression of the ineffable mysteries, of the world beyond sense, that must be entered by the way of sense; and now she believed." [95] Her self was annihilated; old feelings and emotions, inherited loves and hates were destroyed. Her old life had been thrown utterly away.

The mood of spiritual detachment from the corporeal realm is remarkably conveyed, with sufficient suggestion of the worldly to give it meaning and with sufficient intimation of the otherworldly to give it impact. "Without strain or hint of forcing, it contains as much of the authentic Celtic twilight—peace on the wings of the morning—as ever a poem of Senator Yeats." [96] "The Rose Garden" is a miniature gem, intricately carved, delicately handled. It is Machen's most commendable creative achievement with a type of art in which usually only the poets excel.

III *Transcendental Spookery*

By far the most predominant element in Machen's strictly creative works is the weird and occult. As has been observed, his knowledge and his symbols were derived from his childhood environment and from his experience as a cataloger of rare books. One of his catalogs, for example, *The Literature of Occultism and Archaeology*, listed books on ancient worship, astrology, alchemy, animal magnetism, anthropology, assassins, antiquities, ancient history, Behmen and the mystics, Buddhism, clairvoyance, coins, druids, dreams and visions, the divining rod, demonology, ethnology, Egypt, fascination, flagellants, freemasonry, folklore, gnostics, gems, ghosts, Hindus, hieroglyphics and secret writings, herbals, hermetic and other items of a similar nature. For another catalog on alchemy and magic, he wrote a Rabelaisian introduction—anticipatory of Cabell's *Jurgen*—that jumbles with drollery, cabalistic and gnostic symbols, the magician's Heavenly Chaos, the fountain of Spiritual Sol, of Spiritual Luna, of Spiritual Venus, and of Spiritual Mercurius, the tree of the Second Juice, and Queen Sosteris, in an obscure parody of occultism;[97] or, as Machen terms it, this work is an "extravaganza" of occultism based on occult readings and *Le Moyen de Parvenir.*[98]

Despite the preponderance of the pernicious and abnormal among this fantastic array of oddities, Machen's sense of perspective remained relatively unimpaired. He could parody as in *The Spagyric Quest* or treat lightly as in *Don Quijote.* Yet, despite his conscious resistance and unimpaired judgment, he used fifteen of the subjects listed in the above catalog in a more or less prominent manner in his works.

The Great God Pan opens with an experiment in brain surgery, during which the victim of the experiment sees the great god Pan, later gives birth to a daughter, and then dies in a state of hopeless idiocy. The daughter, Helen Vaughan, is farmed out to some people in the country who live near some Roman ruins. She makes frequent sojourns into the woods with two other children, both of whom become mad with terror and shame at what they see there. Helen then disappears for a considerable period of time; later, in London, a trail of ruined men leads to the eventual discovery of her presence. Wherever she lived, she left an aura of evil and the hint of nameless infamies. Finally, Villiers, whose friend had been married to Helen and had committed suicide, by various means learns of her true nature. Villiers takes her a rope with which she kills herself, changing forms many times as she dies, turning from sex to sex, beast to man, man to beast, and beast to hideous protoplasm.

In this tale sensationalism obviously plays a strong role, with a slight tinge of the pseudoscientific and with some symbolism. In a specific sense, the theme might be the attraction and repulsion of evil; but the tale enters Dorothy Scarborough's study in two places—once under the heading of allegorical and symbolical tales of the devil and his allies and once under the category of supernatural biology.[99] She says:

> The most revolting instances of suggestive diabolism are found in Arthur Machen's stories, where supernatural science opens the way for the devil to enter the human soul, since the biologist by a cunning operation on the brain removes the moral sense, takes away the soul, and leaves a being absolutely diabolized. Worse still is the hideousness of *Seeing the Great God Pan,* where the daemonic character is a composite of the loathsome aspects of Pan and the devil, from which horrible paternity is born a child that embodies all the unspeakable evil of the world.[100]

Although in effect Pan may be liberally construed as the devil, Machen had in mind a more general concept calculated to impart the terror of the unknown when he first conceived this experiment in transcendental surgery. He may have derived his symbol from a drawing of the Sabbatic Goat, "a pantheistic and magical figure of the absolute," with a goat's head and feet, wings, woman's breasts, and indescribable eyes, which is neither good nor evil.[101] Waite did not reproduce the plate until 1898, but Machen always kept abreast of his scholarship. The epigraph Machen derived from Knorr von Rosenroth's *Kabala.*[102]

For the second time Machen used the device of the one-thousand-year-old wine in connection with visions of depravity.[103] Also, the atavistic concept of the reversion of evolution, which Machen used later with more telling effect, appeared first in this tale in the account of the death throes of Helen,[104] a process suggesting that embodied in man is the potential to revert instantaneously to the primordial slime from whence he so laboriously and at such great length emerged.

The style is laborious, but the diction is well selected in the effort to render intangible evil tangible and to convey the essence or mood. In all cases Machen leaves the story untold and suggests rather than defines. During the operation, Mary's features become "hideously convulsed." [105] What she has seen is "ineffable, impalpable evil." [106] In the wood Helen Vaughan was seen playing with a " 'strange naked man.' " [107] In London, Herbert, one-time husband of Helen, heard the vilest talk and saw incredible horrors.[108]

Machen, as already noted, enumerated in *Hieroglyphics* the devices which he used to give his work the air of unreality.[109] In *The Great God Pan,* Clarke, who witnessed the experiment in transcendental medicine, began some memoirs fifteen years later to prove the existence of the devil. A portion of the tale is told in those memoirs. The narrative is picked up again in London where Clarke's friend, Villiers, adds to the story by telling what he knows about a collection of pictures, one of which is apparently of Helen, sent to him by the artist Arthur Meyrick. The last part of the tale is conveyed through the papers of Dr. Robert Matheson, who witnessed the disintegration of Helen in her final moments. In other words, the narrative is unraveled by means of indirection. All events are told in retrospect; and, as a consequence, there is no sense of direct conflict or contact between the characters at any given place or at any given moment. The end result is a complete void with respect to the creation of living or "round" characters.

Weygandt imputes that Machen was not a storyteller because his characters were weak, his experience narrow; because he sought moods and atmospheres rather than a character at a crucial moment of life.[110] The charges—no matter how pertinent they may be when applied to the novel form—are neither fair nor relevant, however, in discussion of tales of the weird and supernatural. For as Lovecraft says: "Atmosphere is the all-important thing, for the final criterion of authenticity is not the dovetailing of a plot but the creation of a given sensation. . . . Therefore we must judge a weird tale not by the author's intent, or by the mere mechanics of the plot; but by the emotional level which it attains at its least mundane point." [111]

If Lovecraft's appraisal of this literary genre is true, then any evaluation as to respective merit rests primarily upon the peculiar temperament of the reader. The opinions, therefore, of *The Great God Pan* vary widely. When it first appeared, the reviewers found it too black to stomach[112] and classified it as "weird and ridiculous," "lurid and nonsensical," full of "occult elements," unhealthy, intentionally disagreeable, "an incoherent nightmare of sex," a potboiler, an absurdity. They also regarded it as lacking in elements of terror, in construction, and in character delineation;

as failing in the intention to curdle the blood and to make the flesh creep; and as causing one to shake with laughter instead.[113] The characteristics of the writing were so well defined and, perhaps, obvious that the book evoked two parodies. One by Arthur Rickett, made up like the *Yellow Book* with sketches like Beardsley's, was called the "Yellow Creeper." "R_2OT_3" reacts with "P_4-IFF_5LE" to produce—"'you are approaching the gurgling mysteries, the ghastly, unspeakable, shuddering mysteries that dwell in cheap books.'"[114]

Though the early reviews were in the main unfavorable, the rediscovery of Machen in the 1920's brought various commentaries which were as exaggerated in their praise as the earlier ones had been in their condemnation. Edmund Pearson called Machen the master of the supernatural tale, unsurpassed even by Poe for horror and suggestion of diabolism.[115] Another reviewer stated that Machen's early fiction gave more thrill than Stevenson's. Roberts interpreted the tale further as an "alarming reconstruction of panic," an assessment more in line with Machen's original concept; but he added that Machen wrote from a deep spiritual conviction that evil is persistent and powerful, a concept rare in the 1890's "when men treated sin as a decoration and vice as a degree. I know no artist of the period, except Aubrey Beardsley, who shared Mr. Machen's conviction of the terrible potency of sin."[116] Lovecraft finds the charm of the tale in "the telling, cumulative suspense and ultimate horror," in the "gradual hints and revelations." He admits that the tale is marred by melodrama, that coincidence is stretched; but still Lovecraft derives from the malign witchery an appreciative shudder.[117]

The mounting horror in *The Great God Pan* lacks, however, the personalized, subjective, and psychological impact found in Poe. Machen's use of symbolism throws the emphasis on the idea rather than on a particular situation, and the qualities of fear and dread become accentuated on an expansive intellectual and cosmic plane as opposed to a converging singleness of emotion. Although this tale deals primarily with cosmic fear,[118] it still embodies the underlying philosophy of the tale of supernatural horror as expressed by Lovecraft: "The oldest and strongest emotion of mankind is fear, and the oldest and strongest kind of fear is the fear of the unknown."[119]

The Great God Pan is more modern than the purely Gothic,

and it is less modern than the purely pseudoscientific or psychological tale. The Gothic is outmoded by the collapse of man's belief in witches and demons and vampires, and the pseudoscientific is dated by the rapidity of new discoveries. Only the psychological approach adopted by Poe and his successors retains any great degree of permanency in horror fiction other than as a literary curiosity or as a study in the development of the genre. Machen, although utilizing elements of these three types, introduced symbolism in a Celtic manner to the field of supernatural horror. His symbols are vague enough to avoid identification with temporal superstitions or discoveries, but they are defined well enough to be associated with eternal forces at work in all ages. This symbolism, though it tends to diffuse the sensation so carefully wrought by atmospheric detail, is the unique quality of his work.

Although the element of diabolism, with which Machen was deeply concerned, represents a purely Gothic aspect, he did not look to the early masters of the Gothic for his precedent, nor is his conception of evil simply one of dichotomy of the spirit as typified by Jekyll and Hyde. Actually the machinery of his tale is simply an artifice to waive the barriers which prevent man from seeing the hidden forces of nature. Though the plot bears little resemblance to the work of any earlier writer and though the devices are not clearly purloined from Poe, the consummate skill which Machen displays in the creation of atmosphere and in the power of suggestion compares favorably with that of the American author. There are, however, two distinctions which Machen himself made between his work and Poe's. On viewing Mathern Palace in Gwent, Machen said that it was not quite like the setting of "The Fall of the House of Usher," primarily because the feeling aroused was one of wonder, not terror.[120] Machen admitted that he was remote from Poe in both method and outlook, and he further commented that Poe's terrors are distinct, his own vague and irrational, something like a nightmare.[121]

The truth of the matter is that Machen did not create by immersing himself in a particular mood; he was restricted by his arbitrary definition of literary art to a limited number of ideas and patterns. One of these ideas is that beneath the surface of things lies a hidden world; or, as he puts it, "To the rational man the wasteland is a poor joke; to the super-rational man it is a place of wonder and terrors, fairies and demons." [122] In *The Great God Pan* he accentuates the wonder and the demons; in some of his later tales, the terrors and the fairies.

The second idea which was to him a source of endless fascination is perichoresis—the interpenetration of one age with another.[123] Where Wells looked forward, Machen always looked back.[124] In *Hieroglyphics,* Machen expressed it thus, "it [literature] is the endeavor of every age to return to the first age, to an age, if you like, of savages. . . ." [125] In *The Great God Pan* many slight manifestations of this concept are in evidence: references to the Roman road, ancient ruins, the excavation of a faun or satyr, to wine one thousand years old. One of his characters, Austin, is a collector and an antiquary.[126]

A peculiar manifestation of this overlapping of time with the object of revealing the primordial past is Machen's theory of retrogression which is personified by all the evolutionary forms existing simultaneously in one body and transmuting backwards biologically at the moment of death from human form to protoplasm. This unique theory is more significant in its symbolic than in its romantic impact, but it is obviously additional evidence that Machen's Time Machine worked mainly in reverse.

The significance of *The Great God Pan* with respect to Machen's work as a whole is the experimentation in a field which until that time was completely foreign to him. Although he groaned on reading the completed book and was somewhat aghast at the great gulf between the idea and the fact,[127] the tale was neither so ridiculous as some of the early reviewers would make it, nor so masterful as some of the historians of Gothic fiction imply. As a novice, Machen was learning his trade well. His style was developing in exemplary fashion, and some of the characteristics which came to be a mark of the originality of his genius were present in embryo.

Machen wrote many other tales during the 1890's—such as "The Inmost Light," "The Red Hand," and "The Shining Pyramid"—that are similar to *The Great God Pan* in motif, though in most cases the symbol differed. In every case, however, the symbol signified a dark, fearful, awesome elemental force of nature outside society and beneath the veneer of civilization. This power is not unlike that which one finds at the core of Conrad's *Heart of Darkness,* but Machen has stripped it completely of moral and ethical implications by equating lurid legends of Greek and Roman paganism, druidical rites, and early Christianity. Thus, a bacchanal, a human sacrifice, a black mass, or a witches' Sabbath are all representative of the same underlying concept. Of all of the tales that he wrote during this period, the two works which are the most unique and distinctive are *The Three Impostors* and "The White People."

The Three Impostors was at the same time more slavishly imitative and more original than any work he had written before. The framework of the plot is simply a device, derived directly from Stevenson's *New Arabian Nights,* for linking together a collection of weird tales. Some of them represent, in Lovecraft's estimation, Machen's high-water mark as a terror weaver.[128] The plot, clumsily contrived with no attempt at credibility, centers around Dyson, an armchair supersleuth, to whom the fantastic series of events are gradually revealed, with little detection on his part, and to whom members of Lipsius' gang spin irrelevant tales of horror which constitute the body of the work.

A gold Tiberius, the only one of its kind, coined to celebrate excess, with a faun on the reverse side, has been stolen by Lipsius from Mr. Headley, who is later mummified. Subsequently, a young man named Walters, a member of the gang, pilfers the coin and flees. The search for Walters by the agents of Lipsius is the main thread from which the divergent tales are spun with the ostensible reason of concealing from Dyson the real purpose of the search. Dyson finds the gold Tiberius, Walters' history of the theft, and finally Walters himself, his body tortured with irons and a fire of coals in his middle. The structure of the work has no real literary merit in itself, and the "jaunty Stevensonian manner" somewhat mars the main body of the work.[129]

The original edition of *The Three Impostors* includes "The Novel of the Dark Valley," "The Novel of the Black Seal," "The Iron Maid," not conceived as an intrinsic part of the work, and "The Novel of the White Powder." Later editions include "The Red Hand," written separately for a short story contest. "The Novel of the Dark Valley," a purely Faustian study in diabolism of men who sold their souls for gold, lacks any distinctive qualities worthy of discussion.

The second tale in the book, "The Novel of the Black Seal," a testimony that truth and scientific fact are not synonymous, is narrated by Miss Lally, whose brother was professedly abducted by a deathlike creature with a formless hand and peeled flesh, who had been moldering for years in the grave. Miss Lally had worked for Professor Gregg, an ethnologist, who deciphered a seal, the Sixtystone, and who had journeyed, never to return, to a land of hissing inhuman beings who celebrated "foul mysteries." [130] "The Black Seal" is the first representation of Machen's creative use of elements of folklore strictly Welsh in nature. The commoner facets of Celtic lore, as previously enumerated from a study by Professor Rhŷs, which are to be found in this work are the idea of transmutation, the concept of fairies as dwarfed and cannibalistic creatures, and the references to an unintelligible fairy language. Just as the mother of Helen in *The Great God Pan* conceived her abominable progeny after seeing Pan, so the mother of Jervase Cradock conceived him in the Grey Hills, an area frequented by the Little People. Just as Holmes's Elsie Venner manifests certain snakelike qualities, so Jervase exhibits traits of prenatal heritage in his sibilant speech, the speech of hell, the language of fairies,[131] and in his occasional reversion or transmutation into a reptilian creature.[132]

Two incidental atmospheric details, a murder with a primitive stone weapon and the black seal itself,[133] may have been suggested by archeological discoveries in sites near Machen's home. Both of these were later utilized in "The Red Hand"; and the propensity for cyphers, seals, hieroglyphs, and cuneiform characters is recurrently manifested, though never with the technical competency of Poe.

The next tale "The Novel of the White Powder" also has a pseudoscientific basis, this time the decomposition of a chemical into the powder of *Vinum Sabbati*[134] which induces a physical degeneration more terrifying by far than Dr. Jekyll's private formula. The horrible powder, which first causes the human flesh to burn with a black flame,[135] leaves only the flaming eyes in a formless thing[136] and, finally, "a dark and putrid mass," [137] fully as revolting as the remains of Poe's M. Valdemar or Lovecraft's "Thing on the Doorstep." By cumulative heaping up of atmospheric detail, the dissolution becomes an overwhelming symbol of all evil and hideous corruption,[138] of the witches' Sabbath and devilish doings, and of the infernal sacraments.[139] The discrediting of mesmerism, spiritualism, materializations, and theosophy[140] serves to accentuate the horror of underlying forces beyond the scope even of those occult sciences.

The thread of *The Three Impostors* then leads back to Lipsius and his gang, who drink wine of the Red Jar of Avallaunius—the wine of fauns—and indulge in strange rites and unwholesome orgies.[141] The ending, with Dyson and Phillips finding Walters' tortured remains in a dark room—the ceiling of which, covered with festering and pustuled Cupids, resembled a dance of death—[142] presents an incongruous tone of ghastly humor, as if Machen were admitting a feeling of intellectual guilt for having written such nonsense.

The predominant elements of the tales in *The Three Impostors* are demonism or omnipresent evil, symbolically conveyed; the superstitions of folklore treated as a living reality; pseudo-scientific devices, or "supernatural science," as Scarborough prefers, in the field of uncanny chemistry;[143] and the armchair detective, whose main ability lies in decoding cyphers and listening to weird tales. As far as the first of these, omnipresent evil, is concerned, Machen's preoccupation with sin does not quite resolve itself simply into Faustian villains. In fact, Machen seems not to have been concerned with villains at all; for, as Philip Van Doren Stern says, he deals primarily "with the elemental forces of evil, with spells that outlast time, and with the malign powers of folklore and fairy tale." [144] The determination to express "transcendental beastliness" almost assumes the form of an obsession: "Mr. Machen's literary monomania takes the form of postulating that behind the veil of matter, in the centre of the material universe, resides an obscene and terrible power, the revelation of which brings to mortals infamy and madness." [145] The common motif in the lust of the men in "The Dark Valley" who sold their souls to the devil, in the diabolical scientific experiment in "The Inmost Light," in the survival of a malignant and bestial race in "The Black Seal" and "The Red Hand," and in the infernal chemical of the witches' Sabbath in "The White Powder" is the symbolic representation of the forces of evil:

Through it threads the theme, that of nearly all his tales, of the disintegration of a soul through an encounter with the mysteries which we are forbidden to know, the Sabbatic revels, the two-horned goat, alchemy, devil-worship, and the eternal and indescribable symbols. The problem is always the same, that of facing the great God Pan and the danger that lurks for the man who dares the facing.[146]

Although Machen later satirized the Puritans who scorned his work for lack of a moral, one reviewer jokingly pointed out that the censure was too harsh because the Puritans also had a lively sense of the demoniac.[147] The thesis that the "Bacchic cultus and Panic lechery survive" [148] is handled in such a way that a moral from the modernized Faust element can barely be inferred in the diffuse impression of horror and retribution, stronger in "The Novel of the White Powder" than in any other of these tales.[149] Even so, in that tale the drug is taken by chance so that the nonmoral theme falls into a moral gulf.[150] The emphasis is upon sensationalism.

The second predominant element, though actually but a separate symbol to convey diabolism and nameless evil, is folklore. Quite apart from his mythological machinery and his archeological, paleontological, and ethnological references, Machen's use of legends of the *Daione Sidhe* of Ireland and *Tylwyth Teg* of Wales is an outstanding feature of his work. The demoniac notions of the Little People in "The Black Seal" and in "The Red Hand" incorporate the superstitions of transmutation, of a dreadful lore, and of a living fear—all so characteristic of the Celtic mind. Although Sheridan Le Fanu had written of vampires in *Carmilla* some years previously and although Yeats, Lady Gregory, and Dunsany were contemporaneously revitalizing Irish drama and poetry with Irish legend, Machen was without predecessor in his use of Celtic lore in tales of supernatural horror. Dorothy Scarborough devoted a considerable portion of her study to this aspect of the supernatural: "Comparative study of folklore, with the activities of the numerous associations, has brought to light fascinating material." [151] "Ambrose Bierce, Bram Stoker, F. Marion Crawford, and Arthur Machen have written a number of stories bringing out this side of ghostly psychology, showing the bands of outlawed spirits that prey on society." [152] Dorothy Scarborough's analysis of Machen's use of the folk tale points out the following qualities: the "strange, sinister aspects," the "ageless evil," the "loathsome fairies," the "obscene dances," and the "vast ages of enigmatic power," all of which make one want to "rinse his mind out after reading. . . ." [153] She evidently had in mind a recollection of Jervase Cradock in "The Black Seal" when she wrote: "Arthur Machen's stories have an effect like a slimy trail of some loathly beast or serpent." [154]

The pseudoscientific element, by Machen's time, had almost become a separate field of literature. As Bailey points out, "On every side, scientific fiction overlaps other kinds. . . . The most fantastic tale of terror may exhibit its scientific formulas." [155] The scientific and supernatural horror tale merged in the decline of the pure Gothic when science began to supersede superstition and the devil-fearing form of Christianity. In earlier times, however, such works as *The Arabian Nights* and Apuleius's *Golden Ass* may be considered as forerunners of scientific fiction.[156] In the modern sense, *Frankenstein* really is the milestone which Balzac, Hawthorne, Poe, Stevenson, Doyle, Wells, Bierce, and numerous contemporary authors have passed long since. The pseudoscientific elements in Machen's *The Great God Pan* and *The Three Impostors* are obvious enough to place Machen firmly within this group; yet the truly scientific aspects are so tenuous, vague, and superficial as to produce only secondary or incidental effects.

In the final analysis, however, *The Three Impostors* approaches the norm of the structure and method of scientific fiction closely enough for serious consideration. The plot is a story within a story; the opening, a commonplace setting with the discovery of a manuscript or seal, in Machen's case always of a cryptic nature; and the ending, the loss or destruction of the secret by means of the disappearance or death of the character cognizant of the secret.[157] The method deviates somewhat from the point of view of the single "veracious" person,[158] though Machen often corroborates the testimony with a coroner's report. Finally, Machen's chief interest was in ideas rather than in people, which is in accord with Bailey's findings: "The interest of scientific fiction is chiefly in things, ideas, and discoveries, rather than in people." [159]

The last element of *The Three Impostors*, that of the supersleuth, is so lacking in depth of characterization as to be scarcely worth mentioning. The scholarly Dyson seldom acts as more than a cryptographer and as a willing audience to incredible tales. Only once, in "The Red Hand," does he capture a culprit. Instead of establishing character by means of distinctive conversation, Machen used the stilted, conventional Victorian dialogue. His detectives "speak like books." [160]

Dorothy Scarborough went so far as to state that F. Marion Crawford's *The Dead Smile* and some of Arthur Machen's tales have a "Russian horror,"[161] a term which would have roused Machen to an endless harangue had he been aware of it. Despite the obvious literary parallels, Machen claimed the division of personality in "The White Powder" as original with him; he acknowledged no borrowing other than the powder of the witches' Sabbath from Payne Knight. And as for the belief that the Little People were pre-Celtic inhabitants, he did not acknowledge a source but admitted that the idea was not his, at the same time avowing that the idea of their continued existence was his.[162]

Although these tales have usually been categorized as demonology and sensational horror stories and have been analyzed as accentuating the horror and thrill,[163] Machen was concerned in the main—as the previous chapters of this book clearly show—with the thesis that the hieroglyphs of man's heritage (the apocrypha and legends and lore), to those who read them aright reveal awful, unspeakable, and inexpugnable forces of nature, which the bodies of organized knowledge (such as history, science, and theosophy) tend to de-emphasize. His demons are, therefore, not "demons" in the ordinary sense of the word; the horror is not horrible; nor the thrill sensational when the intent of the tales is kept in mind. By virtue of literary necessity, he could only use the methods and techniques long established in the field of the supernatural, the veiled suggestion and atmospheric tension; but "he never, in the terror tales, describes the erotic and rarely the horrible."[164]

As one would expect in tales of cosmic forces of frightening proportions, the atmosphere is more convincing than anything that happens.[165] One critic, calling Machen an adept in the art of elusiveness, states that he deals in ancient mysteries and hints at the macabre, the sinister, the unspeakable: "His puppets peep and mutter through an atmosphere of forbidden knowledge and obscure rites of remote antiquity, which he would seem to suggest are not as remote as they ought to be."[166] Van Vechten's expression of the atmospheric effects produced by "this delver in forgotten lore" is rhapsodical:

Machen evokes beauty out of horror, mystery, and terror. He suggests the extremes of the terrible, the vicious, the most evil, by never describing them. His very reserve conveys the infinity of abomination. . . . He knows so much, indeed, that he is able to say nothing. He keeps the thaumaturgic secrets as the alchemists were bidden to do. Instead of raising the veil, he drops it. Instead of revealing, he conceals. . . . He must have encountered the horror himself and yet he lives to ask the riddle in flowing prose! [167]

One reviewer captures much of the spirit of the tales by considering them in retrospect: "What one remembers after reading is what one remembers from long ago: the magnificent feeling for lonely and forbidding places, the scenes of ancient evil; the preoccupation with the sinister world which for Machen lays always under the daily surface; the dimness of characterization; and the long-drawn-out unclimactic climaxes of horror seen through a glass darkly." [168]

Though opinions varied widely on the overall significance of these tales, many critics had a kind word for Machen's stylistic ability in the creation of atmospheric effects. To sum up, two of these so-called novels, "The White Powder" and "The Black Seal," have the symbol and the thesis sufficiently subordinated to produce horror which is not exclusively on a transcendental or cosmic plane. In the merger of the many facets of his writing, these two stories emerge as outstanding works of supernatural horror; "The White Powder" approaches the absolute combination of loathsome fright[169] when Wyn Leicester, "still living and malevolent, deliquesces through the floor." [170] "The Black Seal" becomes equally horrifying, subordinating the nauseating to a greater effect, when the idiot boy's back shoots out a "snaky pseudopod." [171] This "infinity of abomination" finds no counterpart in literature save in "The Elixir of Life" and in "The Case of M. Valdemar"; and in the mixture of horror, witchery, and terror, in the "brooding atmosphere of dread, he [Machen] succeeds better than any other in imparting fear of the unknown." [172]

Although Machen employed what Dorothy Scarborough refers to as "dream supernaturalism" in *The Hill of Dreams,*[173] he did not produce another notable work purely in the weird and occult genre until 1899 in "The White People," which he professed to have composed from "odds and ends of folklore" mixed with pure inventions.[174] In the long expository prologue he explains more definitively than anywhere else what he considers to be the nature of sin and holiness: "'Sorcery and sanctity . . . these are the only realities. Each is an ecstasy, a withdrawal from the common life.'"[175] Sin he describes as "'an esoteric, occult thing,'"[176] "'the taking of heaven by storm. . . .'"[177] "'[Holiness] is an effort to recover the ecstasy that was before the Fall. But sin is an effort to gain the ecstasy and the knowledge that pertain alone to angels, and in making this effort man becomes a demon.'"[178]

The story of "The White People" is one of unconscious sin where a little girl innocently becomes a devil worshiper because of her nurse who is a witch.[179] The story is revealed through the diary of the girl in which she records, in naïve fashion, all of her strange secrets—Nymphs; Dôls; Jeelo; voolas; Alala; the White, Green, and Scarlet Ceremonies; the Xu language; water like wine; and the white people.[180] Interspersed in this *Arabian Nights* atmosphere[181] of old languages, queer tunes, wine, extraordinary games, and images,[182] are the tales which the nurse told the child as a part of the bewitching process: the story of a girl with a demon lover;[183] of a man loved by the queen of fairies;[184] and of Lady Avelin, a witch and snake-woman, finally burned at the stake, who worshiped the glame stone, kept a wax doll, which turned into a handsome young lover at night, and destroyed four of her five bachelor suitors by means of effigies.[185] After the child became proficient at turning tables over by magic, she poisoned herself, before she had time to transmit the evil to others, in front of a white, luminous Roman statue.[186]

The prologue to "The White People" illustrates in an expository manner Machen's indisputable interest in the two unfathomables—the supernal and the infernal, White Magic and Black Magic.[187] The tale itself draws a subtle distinction between the two, delicately cloaking Machen's "almost unlimited power in the intimation of potent hideousness and cosmic aberration"[188] in a weird, uncanny beauty which lends the appearance of White Magic, but is, in reality, Black Magic. Lovecraft ranked the tale above Machen's other work in the field of supernatural horror as finer in atmosphere and in general artistic value but as less famous and simpler in plot. He found in the "marvellous vividness," in the "dimly disquieting" atmosphere, in the "triumph of skilful selectiveness and restraint," and in the evil of the witches' Sabbath revealed through childish prattle and juvenile naïveté a "masterpiece of fantastic writing." He further felt that Machen cast an imaginative spell which added weirdness, strangeness, and the suggestion of grotesque sentience.[189]

"The White People" bears considerable semblance to Machen's earlier works; but in fact, the theme of evil with an attraction so great as to ensnare innocence—not in the ordinary but in the extraordinary sense—finds no counterpart in literature except in Milton's *Paradise Lost,* though, of course, the occult approach is vastly different from the epic. "Machen sees evil as most men see good, a caress pleasant but perilous to those who are not masters of their fate." [190] Machen's usual tendency toward the esoteric shows through in this as in other tales, but here he concentrates his efforts toward the creation of atmosphere and of descriptive passages of secret places of nature.

Aside from an occasional tale, the idea for which may have been conceived in the nineteenth century, Machen never allowed sin and evil to emerge triumphant after "The White People." Just as *The Hill of Dreams* represents the crystallization of his symbolic traits, so "The White People" is his masterpiece of supernatural horror; and just as most of his other tales normally do not convey horror in the physical sense, so this tale also deals only with cosmic horror. The deliberate delicacy and finesse with which he draws the fine distinction between good and evil is the most remarkable attribute of the work. Only with the growing sense of the nature of sin on the part of the narrator is the reader able to detect signs of Black Magic behind the veil of uncanny beauty, and only with the child's self-destruction does the conclusion become irrevocable. Furthermore, the simple language which Machen uses to simulate childish prattle and to produce the effect of naïveté creates a verisimilitude unparalleled in his other works. Barring the long prologue, which is alien expository matter in an artistic sense, "The White People" is his most polished work in this genre. It is a coherent fragment which Machen could not sustain or enlarge into the Great Romance.

If space permitted, a complete review of Machen's works would show that he bordered on the weird and occult in a major portion of his works; yet it was not until he became an unwilling journalist that he found the opportunity and the incentive to turn out works purely supernatural in nature. Representative of this group and the first in the genre is "The Bowmen," the plot of which is very simple. Under the guise of wartime censorship restrictions, Machen, lacking firsthand knowledge of the battlefront, avoided factual data entirely; and its absence accentuated the atmosphere of the supernatural with which he was concerned. In a hopeless situation the British soldiers kill ten thousand Germans when one man invokes the aid of an occult being who brings succor in the form of celestial armies.

The tale itself is a very slight one, couched in the vaguest language; yet, printed as it was at a critical moment in wartime, it aroused considerable comment. When "The Bowmen" was first published in book form along with other stories of supernatural dreams and visions, Machen analyzed many of the rumors and opinions which he felt had resulted from the publication of his tale. Actually he had conceived of the celestial succor as Welsh saints who conjured up the archers of Agincourt, mercenaries from Gwent.[191] The editor of *The Occult Review* had written to him in reference to the tale, and "The Bowmen" had been reprinted in several parish magazines. The crux of the matter, as Machen saw it, was that his "long line of shapes with shining about them" became in the May issue of *The Occult Review* "a row of shining beings," which were assumed to be angels.[192] Later collections therefore include "The Bowmen" under the title of "The Angels of Mons." Furthermore, in a postscript to the first edition, Machen expresses his incredulity over an account in the August issue of *The Occult Review* of a soldier who professed to have seen a vision of St. George aiding him in battle.

In rebuttal to Machen's statements, Harold Begbie wrote that the angels appeared to the soldiers in France even before Machen wrote "The Bowmen." Moreover, he thought Machen to be a hypocrite, and flippant about serious matters.[193] Begbie, an occultist, believed in telepathy[194] and expressed with conviction that one day man would commune with the dead.[195] Ralph Shirley, the editor of *The Occult Review,* also wrote a rebuttal to Machen's statement that "The Bowmen" was purely fictional.[196] The tale also elicited a parody by T. W. H. Crosland called "Find the Angels" and subtitled "The Showmen: A Legend of War." Such reactions encouraged the publishers to reissue "The Bowmen" in 1915 with an enlarged postscript further discussing apparitions and vision stories as hallucinations. Machen continued to aver that his tale was the cause of the hullabaloo: "The gossip, as I still believe, derived proximately or remotely from the story of 'The Bowmen.' "[197]

At the time of publication of "The Bowmen" Machen did not feel completely sure of the nature of the phenomena arising from it; but by 1922, he had no hesitancy in referring to such episodes as mass illusion[198] or mob emotion.[199] One critic stated in connection with the tales included in *The Bowmen and Other Legends of War:* "As the beginning of an interesting 'mythos' they will have a permanent place in the literature of the war."[200] Even Dorothy Scarborough classifies "The Bowmen" under the heading of "Supernatural Life" as a legend due to the influence of war.[201] The reviewer for *The Dial,* however, had a somewhat different interpretation: "Such tales of celestial succor seem to have spread from one end of the Anglo-French battle-line to the other, and it appears more likely that they are all traceable to the peculiar horror, the stupendous magnitude and unspeakable awfulness, of the titanic struggle than to any single invention."[202] Machen himself, though he preferred to take credit for the origin of most of the stories of similar nature arising on the battlefield, did not discount the possibility of miraculous intervention, but he believed that in this case none existed.[203]

Although Albrecht classifies Machen as an important writer of supernatural fiction,[204] his tales in this genre are extremely similar in nature and very fragile at best; and, for purposes of further analysis, they should be kept distinct from his tales of cosmic horror, which may prove to bring him lasting fame. "The Bowmen" is significant in one sense, however. After that time Machen turned more to marvelous visions and away from infernal machinations.

In 1916, Machen turned out a weird and occult tale of quite a different texture than anything he had done before. *The Terror* deals with the revolt of animals against man when they sense that he is not king. Daphne du Maurier's "The Birds,"[205] adapted for radio production in 1953 and for cinema in 1962, with its cumulative effect of malevolence and terror, may have been suggested by Machen's original tale. For several seemingly unrelated episodes of men being destroyed apparently inadvertently by insects, fowls, or beasts, many possible theories and explanations are offered which are weird and occult in nature. The one which has the greatest efficacy is the discovery by the Huns of a

Z-ray, a kind of psychic "aether" which has the power to alter the form of material objects from a distance.[206] The final explanation, the rebellion of the entire animal kingdom against man, is more weirdly rational than any of the wildest conjectures offered as misleading clues in the great mystery.

Jordan-Smith calls *The Terror* "a better yarn than most of Poe's mystery tales. . . ."[207] Another commentator describes the tale as a forthright mystery steadily cumulative in intensity with no subplots and a denouement as highly ingenious as Wells's *War of the Worlds*—perhaps more so because it has philosophic implications unexpected in a story of this type.[208] Although *The Terror* contains elements of ratiocination and although the occult elements could scarcely be considered on the ghostly or supernatural side, it is one of the most striking proofs of Machen's originality in the fabrication of ideas not impossible in the realm of belief but still highly divorced from reality. In relation to the sum total of his works, it is unique; and, when compared with his other works in the genre of the weird and occult, it has plot and substance rather than the airy nothings in his dream-vision tales. It is a modern mystery story, except on an entirely different level. In it Machen expressed creatively one of his favorite expository themes: the distinction between man and animal, namely spirituality versus rationality.[209]

Most of Machen's fictional work either bordered on the weird and occult or contained occult references and allusions. This chapter has dealt only with the tales purely in the genre. Even so, they are in their entirety exceedingly repetitious in theme, but they represent a voluminous portion of his work. His first successful publication was in this area, and he continued to be creative in this field alone until 1936 when *Children of the Pool,* his last anthology, appeared. From 1927 through 1931, he had written a tale a year for Cynthia Asquith's anthologies. The tales discussed in this chapter, however, are sufficient to elucidate all of the varied facets of his talent in this particular field and to ensure a representative coverage of style and theme.

CHAPTER 5

A Grain of Wheat

THE impelling motive of Machen's life was the psychological need to write. He wrote long before he had anything to say and long after he had said all that he had to convey. He wrote on menus; he wrote for church programs; he wrote advertising booklets; he wrote for magazines and newspapers; he wrote voluminously to his many correspondents; but, above all, he wrote to please himself. His work took the form of filler, reviews, criticism, journalism, letters, formal essays, personal essays, satire, autobiography, prose poems, sketches, rhymed poetry, fantasy, tales of horror and the supernatural, strange tales, and romances of all sorts; but he avoided drama because he could not create direct conflict or living characters, and he only skirted the novel form because he was on principle opposed to realism. When asked if Mr. Machen was not the greatest living novelist, the editor of *The Academy* replied that Mr. Machen is a writer of romances, not a novelist. In the former category he stands alone.[1] Without doubt, his strongest desire was to create the Great Romance; but, since his efforts constantly fell below his expectations in this respect, he tried varied forms of writing in a continuous effort to realize his secret yearning: immortality in the field of literature.

Similarly, for the same reason, he fitted various styles to the sundry forms. His translations are revealing of his linguistic versatility, his ability to retain the authentic savor of the original in both content and style. In various of his works he imitated Rabelais, Burton, Poe, Stevenson, Coleridge, and Lamb; but in *The Hill of Dreams,* where he made a concerted effort to be entirely original, his style is distinctly uneven and ranges from unmoving and lifeless language to magnificent intonation. Though he tried both naturalistic and reportorial style, his easiest and most natural means of expression, which he could write without apparent effort and which he used in his letters and personal essays, retained some echoes of the seventeenth century, as Lamb's did—faint archaisms, copia, scholastic logic, and quotations from Latin, French, Welsh, and seventeenth-century English authors. Though a great portion of his life was spent in hack work as translator, cataloger, advertiser of rare books, proofreader, reviewer, reporter, and columnist or featured writer, his work is almost always recognizable (except for sheer filler), even when it is unsigned, so great is the air of distinction which he gives it. In view of the unusual volume of his literary output, it is commendable that, though most of his work received a severe lashing at the hands of one reviewer or another, even his worst detractors have given him credit for being a great stylist.

Several marked influences upon Machen's work have been noted. Most important according to all evidence, including his own statement, was the environment of early childhood—wild Wales, where folklore, legend, Christianity, and the remains of the Roman occupation all merge with the natural setting to form a living, yet historical reality and to provide the food upon which mysticism is nurtured. This background provided the setting and symbolism for most of his creative works which are likely to endure. The second large influence, which shaped, to a considerable extent, his literary attitude and philosophy, was the influence of writers of the Romantic, early Stuart, and medieval periods of English literature—periods which, in effect, stand in contradistinction to Rationalism, Materialism, and outward expansion. From the Romantic period—to which Machen was linked as a conscious follower of Stevenson—Poe, Coleridge, De Quincey, and Lamb directly influenced Machen's work; Hawthorne, indirectly; Keats and Wordsworth were often quoted. From the seventeenth century, Burton was a direct influence; and Browne was often quoted. From the later medieval period and early Renaissance, Malory and Rabelais were the two chief sources of inspiration; and references to the early alchemists, mystics, occultists, and magicians frequently appear as do references to demonology and witchcraft. *The Mabinogion* and *Arabian Nights* provide a large portion of the imagery.

Although Machen was not consciously a part of any intellectual movement of his own time, certain echoes nonetheless persist of the French Symbolists—particularly of Huysmans, Baudelaire, and

Maeterlinck; and of the "art for art's sake" group—namely Pater and Wilde. Though a certain amount of the *fin de siècle* spirit is evident in Machen's writing, his rebellion against Victorian reticence was not strong enough, not bold enough to place him securely in their ranks. The training of his youth kept him bound somewhat to the Church, and his works always have a spiritual import.

Despite all of these influences, Machen's works bear the mark of a highly, strangely original mind. Since he was not gifted with a fertile imagination and was too reserved to gain the necessary experience from living, he repeated himself with great frequency and thus limited his chances of survival as an author by refusing to build upon borrowed plot situations and characters. A third influence which had considerable effect on shaping his writing was that of journalism. Producing continually for journals tended to shape the material in terms of space so that Machen never really learned the techniques of unity and organization necessary to a longer and more sustained work.

Of the various elements of Machen's works, the spirit of romanticism is the most pervasive. All of his works are imbued with it, even his expository essays and his satire, which either defend the thesis of the real world hidden beneath the surface or attack the naturalistic opponents of that thesis. Symbolism also abounds in a great portion of his works, but only *The Hill of Dreams* is systematically symbolistic. Primarily, the element of mysticism enters his work extensively after 1899. Those works exclusively mystical are too esoteric to hold a following and, to all practical appearances, are now dead. His tales in the weird and occult genre are the most extensive of his purely fictional works; and, though he considered them potboilers, they are the most likely to survive. Since they are fairly short, he was able to sustain unity and atmosphere; since he wrote them to amuse and entertain himself, the reader is more likely to be entertained than he is by a serious mystical or symbolic theme; and though they are less metaphysical than some of his work, they still have a certain cosmic significance which prevents them from being entirely pointless.

The most typical of the weird facets of his work and the most distinctive are the constantly recurrent themes which he obtained from the living folklore of Wales: dwarfish, wizened, and malignant fairies; the unintelligible languages and speaking with tongues; transformations and transmigrations; and the hint of cannibalistic rites among the Little People. This aspect of Machen's work is most uniquely his own. He has turned local color into symbols of universal meaning and application. His work in this field differed in two respects from that of his predecessors: first, in the use of Celtic legend; second, in the de-emphasizing of physical manifestations of terror in favor of the psychical. The real impact of his tales of horror and supernatural lies not in their sensational effect but in their transcendental significance. The net result is a humanistic study of the nature of good and evil.

Commenting on *Brave New World,* Machen said that a world without evil would be an unspeakably awful place.[2] His early studies of diabolism and Black Magic suggest that he believed evil to be latent in man and to be held in check only by the moral force; but his evil is always something more vague and terrible than mere earthly transgression. Evil he considered to be that which is completely contrary to the natural order of things, such as a talking dog or animate furniture.[3] Sanctity he considered as the realization of the perfection that was before the Fall, the recovery of the Lost Word, the attainment of the Graal. Certainly he believed that evil is a necessary concomitant to good and that life offers only intimations and hints as to the true nature of both. In other words, Machen was not concerned with the acts of giving candy to children or of cohabiting with prostitutes. His purpose both as an artist and a humanist was to discover, behind the ordinary, the extraordinary and transcendental meaning. Primarily, he was concerned with matters of the soul, with the essence of man, with the paradise lost and never regained, and with the great errantry.

Machen often fails in his fiction in those areas where he cannot resist expounding his thesis instead of introducing it covertly through character or plot or situation. As a creative writer, he was cursed with too much intellectuality. Still, an explicit statement of purpose is an essential element of exposition; and he often embodied his theme in personal essays which dealt whimsically and wittily with life's simple pleasures, with ancient customs, and with the beauties of nature. In formal essays, more scholarly and dogmatic than the personal ones, he presented factually an idea or theory based on research, such as "The Sangraal." But he handled theme less effectively in some tales and fantasies which were primarily concerned with the transcendental nature of good and evil, symbolically portrayed, and with the attainment of sanctity. Machen's satire represented his struggle against the encroachments of materialism upon the world of the spirit; and his satire, like that of Swift, was dictated by strong love of humanity. The enemies of the spirit, as Machen saw them, were big business, industrialization, science, naturalism, democracy, Puritanism, Protestantism, atheism, and Communism. In an age of Materialism, the work of the spirit is largely ignored.

His great weakness as an artist lay primarily in his overreliance on the raw idea. He was too much the scholar, the humanist, the man of letters. Few persons are interested in reading argumentative exposition which consists entirely of a refutation of their way of life. A large portion of his work, mainly contributions to periodicals and newspapers, is thus dated. For the same reason his satires have long since lost their power, if not their validity. In an epoch more favorable to Plato, some of these works might be rediscovered and revived. Machen's hack work written simply to earn a living—advertising "gimmicks," sheer journalism, book reviews, and the like—died the moment it left his pen. On the other hand, the history of English literature is flowered with works, highly divergent in philosophy and completely unsympathetic to an age of Reason or of Materialism, which by virtue of their artistry are still read and appreciated. A few of Machen's works deserve to stand among that group.

Of the works most eligible to survive, his translation of Casanova's *Memoirs* may one day be his chief claim to fame; but the universal aspects of some of his creative works are sufficient to place him above the rank and file even though his genius was particularly limited. In the first place, his work is imbued with the Romantic spirit—the same spirit of discovery of Keats's sonnet "On First Looking into Chapman's Homer" as applied to everyday life and commonplace things in such a manner as to excite the sense of wonder in everything everywhere. In the second place, some of his work imparts joy in the simple pleasures of life, in the beauties of nature, and in love of humanity. Third, the element of mysticism, which through revelation and faith conveys the order and harmony beyond the seeming disorder and chaos, is prominent. Fourth, much of his work develops the sense of historical continuity which links each generation with all ages past.

Finally, his major fictional works present a kind of progressive study of good and evil from pure diabolism to the attainment of sanctity and the occurrence of miracles.

From Machen's voluminous works, few emerge in which the universal qualities enumerated above are conveyed with the consummate artistry to yield a preponderance of critical acclaim and recognition sufficient to place them among the top ranking works of other writers in the same genre. Although even these few works are, generally speaking, second-rate either in execution or idea, they do possess unique qualities deserving of commendation.

The first of these works is *Hieroglyphics,* in which the analysis of four of the world's great books in terms of the principle of ecstasy yields a surprisingly fresh version of their value. Limited though *Hieroglyphics* may be in scope, it presents a disarmingly artful challenge for all those professing interest in fine literature and is deserving of attention by all students today or generations hence. That it is generally ignored by the present generation is in part a measure of the materialistic standards of the modern era, but also attests to the fact that Machen was not creating a new system of literary criticism. He was merely reapplying the impressionistic criticism of Coleridge, De Quincey, and Lamb—an original application of a borrowed idea.

In the same natural style, slightly colloquial and archaic, is Machen's series of essays, *Dog and Duck.* All of the essays follow the same pattern, illustrating that, despite the seeming ingenuousness, they were artfully conceived. His customary hatreds are toned down in harmony with the medium; and what in other works seems no more than rancor and bias becomes in these essays a form of sagacious tolerance humorously conveyed. Machen's talents and knowledge were particularly suited to the personal essay form. These personal essays more nearly represent the true Machen than any of his other works; but in the twentieth century when poets and personal essayists have been greatly ignored and when the art of letter writing and personal essay writing has little currency, he expended most of his efforts on less natural but more remunerative things. Again, as with *Hieroglyphics, Dog and Duck* is more deserving to be read; but, just as in the field of impressionistic criticism, Machen was adapting the style and medium of others to fit his own ideas to such a degree that the works never emerge as unique. No one will ever say "reminiscent of Arthur Machen." Unfortunately, *Dog and Duck* will probably never revive—unfortunately, because pleasure, gusto, and love of humanity are in it; and even more unfortunately, Dog and Duck punch—the dry martini—will probably live on forever.

Of all Machen's attempts at the Great Romance, only *The Hill of Dreams* is worthy of remembering. Although not quite successful as a novel because of the imperfectly fused elements of satire, mysticism, and symbolism, and because of Machen's inability to reproduce conversation and create "round" or living characters, it nonetheless represents his masterpiece in the field of the novel—the fusion of all his standards and ideas in the most perfect manner, the best that he could produce. Though painful in sensation as reawakening adolescence, the novel is important as an experimental work of art foreshadowing the modern stream-of-consciousness school. Like *Tristram Shandy* by which it was suggested, but which it resembles not at all, it stands apart in the field of the novel. It is a *Portrait of the Artist as a Young Man* suggesting a *Ulysses* which Machen did not have the talent to create. His natural limitations restricted him—as Poe's did—to short works: essays, prose poems, sketches, and atmospheric tales.

Machen wrote a volume of mystical prose poems which, it is assumed, were created in the belief that they might one day serve as atmosphere in the Great Romance. Only one, "The Rose Garden," emerges as a work of art complete in itself and produces the feeling of ecstasy resulting from annihilation of the self. It conveys remarkably the loss of substance and resulting spiritual rebirth, and it achieves that rare rapport and harmony necessary to perfect mystical art.

Machen's entire literary output, however, would not suffice to make his name remembered were it not for his tales, frequently reprinted in anthologies of terror and the supernatural. From his voluminous tales in this genre, the following have been selected as the most outstanding and the most representative of some characteristic of his work in the field. *The Great God Pan,* "The Novel of the Black Seal," "The Novel of the White Powder," "The White People," "The Bowmen," and *The Terror.* In *The Great God Pan,* Machen utilizes a set of symbols from Roman mythology to convey diabolism. His idea of perichoresis and instantaneous reversion in the evolutionary cycle is first used in this work and is the most original of Machen's devices. "The Novel of the Black Seal" is centered around the same theme of omnipresent evil, but for the first time he develops a set of symbols from Celtic folklore. The theme of "The Novel of the White Powder" is again diabolization, this time through chemical means. The reversion to primordial slime is as loathsomely described as anything in horror fiction.

"The White People" is a culmination of Machen's ideas of White and Black Magic and also a line of demarcation between his tales of pure diabolism and his tales of the purely supernatural. In this work Machen draws such a fine distinction between sorcery and sanctity that the reader becomes only gradually aware in the atmosphere of uncanny beauty that an innocent soul is being bewitched. A tale told with great finesse and artistry, though less sensational than the others, it is undoubtedly his masterpiece in this field. "The Bowmen," written during Machen's journalistic period, is representative of a block of supernatural tales dealing with miraculous intervention. Written in a reportorial style, it was successful enough in its verisimilitude to arouse controversy as to whether or not the events in the tale actually occurred; it was his only work to sell on a large scale. In wartime, however, such figments seem to seize the imagination of the public much more readily than they do in times of peace; and "The Bowmen," though the best representative of one phase of Machen's writing, appears rather weak today. Another of his war tales, *The Terror*, on the other hand, is again one of his unique masterpieces with universal amplitude. It is a murder mystery in the most modern sense with a spiritual thesis; and the ending, though well prepared for in the beginning, is nonetheless startling in its disclosure.

In terms of the criteria of *Hieroglyphics* some of these works will stand up under criticism as far as idea or conception is concerned. Also, with respect to style, most of them are outstanding. In plot or construction, on the other hand, Machen was extremely weak. However, as he says, the idea is the most important; and a work can live on that alone. His trouble was that he had only a few ideas for all his works; they are stated in slightly different terms but too much resemble one another. At any rate, no one can ever say that he did not achieve withdrawal from common life.

The foregoing résumé of Machen's most significant efforts serves to emphasize that he lacked the temperament, the creative genius to convey the sense of humanity. Thus he was doomed to mediocrity in the field of the novel. Versatile though he was, his natural mediums were the essay and the tale; and the only collection of essays which he wrote which has challenge enough in itself to make us forget for the moment Bacon, Montaigne, or Lamb is *Hieroglyphics*. In the field of the weird and occult, however, he left his mark, a field similarly overcrowded with names more famous than his. His use of pseudoscientific machinations was certainly no innovation. He was preceded by Mrs. Shelley, Stevenson, Hawthorne, and Balzac. His supersleuth was but a feeble imitation of Dupin. Even in the creation of atmosphere he was a lesser Poe.

But, in this respect, Machen's horrors are mainly remote and suggested, seldom physical; and it is precisely in this small area of psychological, transcendental occult that Machen has never been surpassed. His peculiar knowledge of demonology, witchcraft, folklore, particularly Celtic lore, and occult societies and religions fused with his unique talent for suggesting the indescribable through the creation of atmosphere to make him the spokesman without peer for sorcery and sanctity existing always behind the veil of the ineffable mystery. The irony of his fate was that his claim to fame should rest upon his penny dreadfuls instead of upon the Great Romance which he was never able to conceive. He dreamed in fire, but he worked in clay; his desire far exceeded his grasp.

Definite indications of influences on the works of other writers are apparent only in the cases of Lovecraft, Bradbury, Daphne du Maurier, and P. J. Toulet. In the first instance, Lovecraft more than once acknowledges his allegiance to the master;[4] and his "Cthulhu cult" has all the terrible though dimly defined attributes of an outlandish race like Machen's Little People.[5] With Bradbury, however, the link is more tenuous. Few correspondences can be said to exist in the works, but in "The Exiles" Bradbury uses Machen as a character and places him in the company of other masters in the field of fantasy.[6] The similarity to du Maurier is only conjectural and is based upon the single instance of the theme in "The Birds," which is obviously similar to that of *The Terror*. According to Toulet's biographer, Toulet, who translated

The Great God Pan into French, wrote three works which show the influence of Machen—*M. du Paur, La Jeune fille Verte,* and *Contrerimes.*[7] Though no proof has been established, Machen could have had some effect upon the works of Shiel, Richard Middleton, Thomas Wolfe, Proust, and Virginia Woolf; on the first two, in the field of fantasy and weird and occult; and on the others, in his nearly stream-of-consciousness, experimental technique used in *The Hill of Dreams.*

Finally, the indications are strong that Machen may have had a wide spread of submerged ideological effect on the minds of his readers, who were often intellectuals, "Harvard aesthetes"[8] of their own day. Just as he converted Lord Alfred Douglas to Christianity,[9] so he may have turned the minds of others with his spirit of rebellion, his refusal to accept change for its own sake, his Romantic and Idealistic doctrines, his devout religiosity, and his mystical outlook forever bordering on the occult.

In fact, the very diversity of Machen's works and the extent of coverage—for example, his book reviews alone—make it extremely probable that someone will be quoting Machen for generations hence. He skimmed the surface of an infinite variety of human thoughts and deeds in a charming, unusual manner. The main proof concerning Machen's survival, however, still lies in bibliographical study. Lady Benson's opinion to the contrary, Machen could not have had an established literary reputation by 1901. He had only two books published in the 1890's, a few tales in the daily papers and other journals, and a few reviews and essays in *Literature,* mainly unsigned. If he had any reputation at all by 1901, it could only have been bad. In the first decade of the twentieth century when Richards published most of his major work, the sale was little better than that of the average new writer and certainly insufficient to make him popular. Only "The Bowmen" had large sales, and *The Terror* had moderate success by the time of the 1920's. He was, therefore, not rediscovered; he was more literally discovered at a time when the other minor writers of the 1890's, like Maurice Hewlett, who had enjoyed some popularity in his own day, were already forgotten. Since his discovery, Machen has held on well in a limited way. Hundreds of publications by him, about him, or mentioning him were published up to the time of his death.

Since his death, just in the last decade, over one hundred publications have appeared by him, about him, or mentioning him. He finds his following among several groups, and one of these is mystery story addicts. Another group is composed of the book collectors who find in Machen a perpetual challenge because of the seeming endlessness of his published works. Still another embraces the terror and supernatural readers, but enough of the element of the pseudoscientific is present in his tales to attract the more modern group as well. A small body of his readers, ignoring the symbolic implications, see only the pagan element in his works of the 1890's. Such Bohemians form an ever-present following in each succeeding generation. Then, too, Machen has his small occult following which, it seems, he made every effort not to discourage. Only by careful study of his total works does it become clearly evident that he was not an occultist. The true mystics—never a large number in any age—at once sense a kindred spirit in Machen. Among the genuine intellectuals, again a fairly small group, Machen may have some currency; but intellectual fashions change almost as fast as women's hats. At any rate, should the fashion change back to idealism, Machen will still be around, waiting.

Nearly seventy years have elapsed since the first publication of *The Great God Pan*. It is no longer a question of "Will Machen survive?" In a limited but continuing way, he has survived; and when the temper of the times changes, when men once more rebel en masse against the strictures of a Materialistic system and against the Naturalistic movement in literature, publishers are bound to reissue his greater works, because in all literature no more dedicated advocate of tradition, of individuality, of spirituality, of romance and mystery exists than Arthur Machen. In his works lie hidden the soul of a star.

Notes and References

Chapter One

1. Arthur Machen, *Caerleon Edition of the Works* (London, 1923), VIII, 7, hereafter cited as *Works*. All quotations reprinted by permission of The Richards Press, Ltd., and by the Executors of the late Arthur Machen.
2. July 31, 1878, pp. 103, 144, 216; January, 1880, p. 5.
3. *Works*, VIII, 18.
4. *Ibid.*, pp. 86-87.
5. *Ibid.*, p. 105.
6. Henry Danielson, *Arthur Machen A Bibliography* (London, 1923), p. 2.
7. Machen, *Eleusinia* (Hereford, 1881), p. 5.
8. Machen, *Beneath the Barley* (London, 1931), p. 2.
9. Machen, Letter to Henry Savage, Sunday [1921].
10. Munson Havens, ed., *A Few Letters from Arthur Machen* (Cleveland, 1932), p. 11, hereafter cited as *Letters*. All quotations reprinted by permission of The Rowfant Club, 3028 Prospect Avenue, Cleveland 15, Ohio.
11. *Works*, VIII, 117.
12. Machen, *The Anatomy of Tobacco* (New York, 1926), pp. 11-13, hereafter cited as *Anatomy*. All quotations reprinted by permission of Alfred A. Knopf, Inc.
13. *Ibid.*, p. 9.
14. Robert Burton, *The Anatomy of Melancholy* (Philadelphia, 1869), p. 18.
15. *Anatomy*, p. 82.
16. *Ibid.*, p. 183.
17. *Ibid.*, p. 15.
18. *Works*, IX, 12.
19. Machen, *The Chronicle of Clemendy* (New York, 1923), pp. 14-15.
20. Machen, *Precious Balms* (London, 1924), p. 176.
21. Machen, *The Chronicle of Clemendy* (London, 1925), p. 70.

All quotations reprinted by permission of The Richards Press, Ltd., and the Executors of the late Arthur Machen.

22. *Ibid.*, p. 24.
23. *Ibid.*, p. 184.
24. Machen, Letter to A. M. Kennett, May 17, 1892.
25. Machen, *The Chronicle of Clemendy* (New York, 1923), p. 17.
26. Grant Richards, *Memories of a Misspent Youth* (New York, 1933), p. 294.
27. *Works,* IX, 62, 65, 84.
28. *Letters,* pp. 33-37.
29. *Works,* IX, 112.
30. Machen, *The House of Souls* (New York, 1923), p. vii. All quotations reprinted by permission of Alfred A. Knopf, Inc.
31. Machen, *Precious Balms,* pp. 13-26.
32. Machen, *The Hill of Dreams* (New York, 1923), p. vi.
33. *Ibid.*, pp. vi-viii.
34. Henri Martineau, "Arthur Machen et P. J. Toulet Une Correspondence Inédite," *Mercure de France,* CCLXXXI (January 1, 1938), 50.
35. T. Michael Pope, *The Book of Fleet Street* (London, 1930), pp. 144-45.
36. Martineau, *op. cit.*, p. 53.
37. Machen, *House of Souls* (New York, 1923), p. xiii.
38. *Works,* IX, 121.
39. *Ibid.*, pp. 122-39.
40. Lady Constance Benson, *Mainly Players: Bensonian Memories* (London, 1926), pp. 15-18.
41. Machen, "The Benson Company," *Theatre Arts,* XV (September, 1931), 738.
42. *Works,* IX, 108.
43. Machen, *House of Souls* (New York, 1923), pp. viii-xii.
44. *Works,* VI, 99-101.
45. *Ibid.*, p. 94.
46. *Ibid.*, p. 110.
47. Danielson, *op. cit.*, p. 35.
48. St. John Adcock, *The Glory That Was Grub Street* (New York, n. d. 1928), p. 222.
49. Machen, *The Secret Glory* (New York, 1922), pp. xi-xii.
50. *Works,* IV, 157.
51. *Ibid.*, p. 122.
52. *Ibid.*, p. 163.
53. *Ibid.*, p. 147.
54. *Ibid.*, pp. 241-42.

55. *Ibid.*, p. 245.
56. *Ibid.*, p. 170.
57. *Ibid.*, p. 57.
58. *Ibid.*, p. 70.
59. *Ibid.*, pp. 57-58.
60. "Sad Happy Race," *Academy*, LXXIV (June 20, 1908), 903-05.
61. D. P. M. Michael, "The Life and Works of Arthur Machen," unpubl. diss. (University of Wales, 1941), p. 56. All quotations from personal letters reprinted by permission of Janet Davis, daughter of Arthur Machen.
62. Machen, *The London Adventure* (New York, 1924), p. 19. All quotations reprinted by permission of Alfred A. Knopf, Inc.
63. *Ibid.*
64. *Ibid.*, p. 126.
65. Machen, *The Angels of Mons,* 2nd ed. (London, 1915), pp. 52-55.
66. Machen, *War and the Christian Faith* (London, 1918), p. 27.
67. *Ibid.*, pp. 27-28.
68. *Ibid.*, p. 44.
69. *Ibid.*, p. 57.
70. Vincent Starrett, "Arthur Machen and the 'Angels of Mons,'" *Open Court,* XXXII (March, 1918), 191.
71. Covici-McGee Publishers, General letter to the trade, 10 July 1924.
72. Edward Lueders, *Carl Van Vechten and the Twenties* (Albuquerque, 1955), p. 65.
73. Cabell, *Beyond Life in Works* (New York, 1928), I, 201-02.
74. Jordan-Smith, *On Strange Altars* (New York, 1924), p. 231.
75. Lord Alfred Douglas, *Autobiography* (London, 1929), p. 309.
76. *Works,* IX, 175.
77. *Ibid.*, p. 38.
78. Machen, *Dreads and Drolls* (London, 1926), introductory note. All quotations reprinted by permission of The Richards Press, Ltd., and the Executors of the late Arthur Machen.
79. *Ibid.*
80. Machen, Letter to Robert Hillyer, [February 3,] 1927.
81. Bennett Cerf, "Trade Winds: Machen Fund," *Saturday Review of Literature,* XXVI (March 20, 1943), 26.
82. John Gunther, "The Truth About Arthur Machen," *The Bookman,* LXI (July, 1925), 571-74.
83. Cerf, *op. cit.*
84. Machen, Letter to Evans, March 24, 1943.
85. Machen, Letter to John Gawsworth, November 28, 1939.

86. Machen, Letter to Oliver Stonor, August 25, 1947.
87. Machen, Letters to Montgomery Evans, III, December 17, 1946, and May 9, 1947.

Chapter Two

1. William Price Albrecht, "Arthur Machen: A Critical Study," unpubl. diss. (University of Pittsburgh, 1934), p. 21. All quotations reprinted by permission of William Price Albrecht, Chairman, Department of English, University of Kansas.
2. Machen, "Education and the Uneducated," *Academy,* LXXIII (September 14, 1907), 896-900.
3. Machen, *Notes and Queries* (London, 1926), p. 93.
4. Machen, "The Morning Light," *Academy,* LXXIII (July 13, 1907), 676-78.
5. Machen, *The Glorious Mystery* (Chicago, 1924), p. 77.
6. *Works,* IV, 22-23.
7. Machen, *The Shining Pyramid* (London, 1925), Introduction.
8. *Casanova's Escape from the Leads* (New York, 1925), p. 12. Reprinted by permission of Alfred A. Knopf, Inc.
9. *Works,* IX, 94.
10. Machen, "Mandatum Novissimum," *Academy,* LXXIII (September 7, 1907), 866-68.
11. Machen, "False Prophets," *Academy,* LXXV (August 8, 1908), 132-34.
12. Machen, "The Dark Ages," *Academy,* LXXV (July 11, 1908), 36-37.
13. Machen, "New Lamps for Old," *Academy,* LXXV (July 18, 1908), 61.
14. Machen, Letter to Thomas Horan, January 29, 1932.
15. Machen, Letter to Robert Hillyer, November 6, 1925.
16. Machen, Letter to Hillyer, February 25, 1926.
17. Machen, *Notes and Queries,* pp. x-xiii.
18. Machen, *The Glorious Mystery,* p. 214.
19. Machen, Letter to Evans, July 18, 1933.
20. *Authors Take Sides on the Spanish War* (London, 1937), p. 32.
21. Machen, "Farewell to Materialism," *American Mercury,* XXXVI (September, 1935), 49.
22. Machen, Letter to Evans, April 3, 1946.
23. *Ibid.*
24. Machen, "On the Employment of Leisure," *News Letter,* VI (December 22, 1934), 113-14.
25. Machen, Letter to Evans, February 16, 1943.
26. Machen, Letter to Hillyer, September 21, 1931.
27. Albrecht, *op. cit.,* p. 14.

28. William J. T. Collins, *Romance of the Echoing Wood* (Monmouthshire, 1937), p. 3.
29. Machen, *London Adventure* (New York, 1924), p. 86.
30. *Ibid.*, p. 85.
31. Machen, *Dog and Duck* (New York, 1924), p. 132. All quotations reprinted by permission of Alfred A. Knopf, Inc.
32. *Ibid.*, p. 133.
33. *Ibid.*, pp. 150-51.
34. *Ibid.*, p. 154.
35. M. P. Shiel, *The Borzoi 1925* (New York, 1925), p. 165. Carl Van Vechten, *Peter Whiffle* (New York, 1922), pp. 197-98.
36. *Works,* IX, 13.
37. *Ibid.*, pp. 14-15.
38. *Ibid.*, p. 15.
39. Machen, *The Three Impostors* (New York, 1923), pp. x-xviii.
40. Helene Petrovna Blavatsky, *Isis Unveiled* (New York, 1886), I, 162.
41. Machen, *War and the Christian Faith* (London, 1918), p. 46.
42. Machen, "The World to Come," *Academy,* LXXIII (July 27, 1907), 728-30.
43. Machen, *War and the Christian Faith,* p. 46.
44. Machen, *Dog and Duck* (New York, 1924), p. 225.
45. Albrecht, *op. cit.*, p. 19.
46. *Letters,* p. 31.
47. Machen, "The Only Way," *Publisher's Weekly,* CV (February 16, 1924), 512.
48. Machen, Letters to Miss Kurtz, June 20 and September 24, 1934.
49. Machen, "Farewell to Materialism," *American Mercury,* XXXVI (September, 1935), 48.
50. Robert Hillyer, "Up from the Ranks of Grub Street Authorship," *New York Times Book Review and Magazine* (March 4, 1923), p. 21.
51. Machen, *The Green Round* (London, 1933), p. 90.
52. Machen, "Good Little Books," *Academy,* LXXIII (August 10, 1907), 767-68.
53. Machen, " 'Consolatus' and 'Churchmember,' " *Academy,* LXXIII (December 21, 1907), 267-68.
54. *Works,* IV, 170.
55. Machen, *The Secret Glory* (New York, 1922), pp. xi-xii.
56. Machen, "The Sangraal," *Academy,* LXXIII (August 17, 1907), 797-98.
57. Machen, "The Sangraal—II," *Academy,* LXXIII (August 24, 1907), 820-23.
58. Machen, *Notes and Queries* (London, 1926), pp. 72-73.

59. Machen, *London Adventure* (New York, 1924), p. 57.
60. Robert Hillyer, *The Halt in the Garden* (London, 1925), p. iv.
61. *Works,* VIII, 98.
62. Machen, *Dog and Duck* (New York, 1924), p. 199.
63. Machen, *The Shining Pyramid* (Chicago, 1923), pp. 165-66.
64. Machen, *Tom O' Bedlam and His Song* (Westport, Connecticut, 1930), p. 21.
65. *Ibid.,* pp. 34-35.
66. *Ibid.,* p. 46.
67. William J. T. Collins, *The Romance of the Echoing Wood* (Monmouthshire, 1937), p. 2.
68. *Ibid.,* p. 6.
69. Machen, *Bridles & Spurs* (Cleveland, 1951), pp. 69-70. All quotations reprinted by permission of The Rowfant Club, 3028 Prospect Avenue, Cleveland 15, Ohio.
70. *Ibid.,* p. 27.
71. *Letters,* pp. 18-20.
72. Machen, "Farewell to Materialism," *American Mercury,* XXXVI (September, 1935), 43-51.
73. Machen, *The Chronicle of Clemendy* (New York, 1923), p.12.
74. *Works,* VIII, 104.
75. Machen, *Dr. Stiggins* (New York, 1925), p. 11.
76. Machen, *London Adventure* (New York, 1924), p. 16.
77. *Ibid.,* p. 111.
78. *Ibid.,* p. 113.
79. *Ibid.,* p. 26.
80. *Ibid.,* p. 33.
81. *Ibid.,* p. 53.
82. *Ibid.*
83. *Ibid.,* p. 86.
84. Machen, Letter to Evans, October 11, 1945.
85. Machen, *Tom O' Bedlam and His Song,* pp. 21-23.
86. Machen, *Bridles & Spurs,* p. 68.
87. Machen, "Farewell to Materialism," *American Mercury,* XXXVI (September, 1935), 51.
88. Evelyn Underhill, *Mysticism* (London, 1919), Part I, Chapter I.
89. *Ibid.,* Part I, Chapter III.
90. *Ibid.,* pp. 85-86.
91. Mitchell S. Buck, *Afterglow: Pastels of Greek Egypt 69 B.C.* (New York, 1924), pp. 13-15 and 18-19.
92. Machen, *Notes and Queries,* pp. 103-07.
93. *Works,* IX, 80.

Chapter Three

1. *Works,* III, 50-52.
2. *Works,* VIII, 56.
3. *Works,* IV, 12-15.
4. *Anatomy,* p. 9.
5. *Works,* V, 8.
6. Machen, *London Adventure* (New York, 1924), p. 87.
7. Samuel Taylor Coleridge, *Complete Works* (New York, 1871), III, 365.
8. Machen, *The Three Impostors* (New York, 1923), pp. xvii-xviii. Reprinted by permission of Alfred A. Knopf, Inc.
9. Machen, *Glorious Mystery,* p. 69.
10. Coleridge, *op. cit.,* III, 371.
11. *Ibid.,* III, 472.
12. Edgar Allan Poe, "The Poetic Principle," *Works* (New York, 1945), p. 571.
13. *Works,* III, 126.
14. *Works,* V, 141.
15. Machen, *Tom O' Bedlam,* p. 29.
16. Poe, *op. cit.,* p. 573.
17. *Ibid.,* p. 658.
18. Machen, "Edgar Allan Poe—The Supreme Realist," *Glorious Mystery* (Chicago, 1924), p. 86.
19. *Ibid.,* p. 88.
20. Machen, *The Great God Pan* (London, 1916), pp. x-xiii.
21. Robert Louis Stevenson, *Works* (New York, 1918), XIII, 329-30.
22. *Ibid.,* XV, 248.
23. Machen, *London Adventure* (New York, 1924), p. 26.
24. Collins, *Romance of the Echoing Wood,* p. 5.
25. Stevenson, *op. cit.,* XV, 248.
26. *Letters,* p. 26.
27. Collins, *op. cit.,* p. 6.
28. Machen, *Three Impostors* (New York, 1923), pp. vii-viii.
29. Machen, *Hill of Dreams* (New York, 1924), pp. vi-vii. Reprinted by permission of Alfred A. Knopf, Inc.
30. *Letters,* pp. 40-42.
31. Machen, *London Adventure* (New York, 1924), p. 152.
32. Walter Pater, *Selected Works* (London, 1948), p. 549.
33. Pater, *The Renaissance* (Portland, Maine, 1912), p. 300.
34. *Works,* IX, 44.
35. *Works,* III, 129.
36. Machen, *House of Souls* (London, 1906), p. xii.

37. Machen, *Great God Pan* (London, 1916), p. vii.
38. Richard Le Gallienne, *The Romantic '90's* (New York, 1926), pp. 270-71.
39. Coleridge, *op. cit.*, III, 365.
40. Frederick Carter, *The Dragon of the Alchemists* (London, 1926), p. 6.
41. *Ibid.*, p. 7.
42. Machen, *House of Souls* (London, 1906), p. xi.
43. Joseph Wood Krutch, "Tales of a Mystic," *Nation*, CVX (September 13, 1922), 258.
44. *Ibid.*
45. William Blake, *Poems and Prophecies* (London, 1927), p. 333.
46. Collins, *op. cit.*, pp. 5-6.
47. Krutch, *op. cit.*, p. 259.
48. *Works*, IX, 69.
49. Machen, *The Shining Pyramid* (Chicago, 1923), p. 136.
50. G. Turquet-Milnes, *The Influence of Baudelaire* (New York, n. d.), p. 219.
51. *Works*, V, 24.
52. *Works*, II, 180.
53. Pater, *Selected Works*, p. 43.
54. *Ibid.*, p. 463.
55. *Works*, III, 116.
56. Turquet-Milnes, *op. cit.*, pp. 250-53.
57. *Works*, II, 173.
58. Underhill, *Mysticism* (London, 1919), p. 87.
59. *Ibid.*, p. 93.
60. *Ibid.*, p. 94.
61. *Ibid.*, p. 151.
62. *Ibid.*, p. 154.
63. *Ibid.*, p. 163.
64. *Ibid.*, pp. 167, 177.
65. *Ibid.*, p. 126.
66. *Ibid.*, p. 117.
67. *Ibid.*, Part I, Chapter V.
68. *Ibid.*, Part I, Chapter VII.
69. *Ibid.*, pp. 203-04.
70. *Ibid.*, p. 216.
71. *Ibid.*, p. 219.
72. *Ibid.*, p. 535.
73. *Works*, IV, 57.
74. Machen, *Beneath the Barley* (London, 1931), pp. 2-3.
75. Vincent Starrett, *Buried Caesars* (Chicago, 1923), p. 1. All quotations reprinted by permission of the author.

76. Lady Constance Benson, *Mainly Players: Bensonian Memories* (London, 1926), p. 163.
77. Casanova de Seingalt, *Memoirs* (New York, 1925), translator's note.
78. Machen, *The Three Impostors* (New York, 1923), pp. x-xviii.
79. John Rhŷs, *Celtic Folklore: Welsh and Manx* (Oxford, 1901), I, 262-63.
80. *Ibid.*, I, 276.
81. *Ibid.*, I, 277.
82. *Ibid.*, II, 607.
83. *Ibid.*, II, 615.
84. *Ibid.*, II, 671.
85. *Ibid.*, II, 673.
86. *Ibid.*, II, 674-79.
87. Machen, Letter to Howard Wolf, March 15, 1941.
88. Basil Davenport, "The Devil Is Not Dead," *Saturday Review of Literature,* XIII (February 15, 1936), 4.
89. William W. Watt, *Shilling Shockers of the Gothic School* (Cambridge, Massachusetts, 1932).
90. Dorothy Scarborough, *The Supernatural in Modern English Fiction* (New York, 1917), pp. 71-72.
91. Arthur Rickett, *Lost Chords: Some Emotions Without Morals* (London, 1895), p. 18.
92. Machen, *Precious Balms,* p. 9.
93. Cornelius Weygandt, *A Century of the English Novel* (New York, 1925), pp. 43-44.
94. *Ibid.*, p. 330.
95. Machen, Letter to Evans, April 3, 1946.
96. Paul Jordan-Smith, *On Strange Altars* (New York, 1924), p. 227.
97. Machen, *The Angels of Mons,* 1st ed. (London, 1915), p. 11.
98. Weygandt, *op. cit.*, p. 438.
99. Machen, Letter to Howard Wolf, March 4, 1931.
100. Scarborough, *op. cit.*, p. 251.
101. Machen, *London Adventure* (New York, 1924), pp. 28-29.
102. J. O. Bailey, *Pilgrims Through Time and Space* (New York, 1947), p. 72.
103. *Ibid.*, p. 123.
104. Edward Wagenknecht, ed., *When I Was a Child* (New York, 1946), pp. 272-73.

Chapter Four

1. *Letters,* p. 7.
2. *Works,* V, 5-9.

3. Machen, "Unconscious Magic," *Literature*, II (January 29, 1898), 112-13.
4. *Works*, V, 17.
5. *Ibid.*, p. 18.
6. *Ibid.*
7. *Ibid.*, p. 43.
8. *Ibid.*, p. 18.
9. *Ibid.*, pp. 22-23.
10. *Ibid.*, p. 48.
11. *Ibid.*, p. 66.
12. *Ibid.*, pp. 94-97.
13. *Ibid.*, pp. 91-93.
14. *Ibid.*, p. 125.
15. *Ibid.*, pp. 34-35.
16. *Ibid.*, p. 38.
17. *Ibid.*, pp. 38-39.
18. *Ibid.*, pp. 43-60.
19. *Ibid.*, p. 46.
20. *Ibid.*, p. 60.
21. *Ibid.*, p. 64.
22. *Ibid.*, p. 47.
23. *Ibid.*, pp. 57-58.
24. *Ibid.*, p. 24.
25. *Ibid.*, pp. 65-68, 74, 84.
26. *Ibid.*, p. 84.
27. *Ibid.*, pp. 98-99.
28. *Ibid.*, pp. 105-22.
29. *Ibid.*, p. 123.
30. *Ibid.*, p. 126.
31. *Ibid.*, pp. 136-39.
32. *Ibid.*, pp. 141-66.
33. *Ibid.*, p. 54.
34. *Ibid.*, p. 168.
35. Danielson, *Arthur Machen A Bibliography*, p. 31.
36. Machen, *Precious Balms*, pp. 37-51.
37. *Ibid.*
38. *Ibid.*, p. 48.
39. C. Lewis Hind, *More Authors and I* (New York, 1922), p. 201.
40. "The Notebooks of Arthur Machen," *Times Literary Supplement*, XXI (March 9, 1922), 155.
41. August Derleth, "A Note on Arthur Machen," *Reading and Collecting*, I (November, 1937), 7.
42. R. Ellis Roberts, "Arthur Machen," *Sewanee Review*, XXXII (July-September, 1924), 356.

43. Danielson, *op. cit.*, pp. vii, ix.
44. *Anatomy,* pp. 14-15.
45. *Letters,* p. 48.
46. Machen, *Dog and Duck* (New York, 1924), p. 40.
47. *Ibid.*, pp. 47-52.
48. *Ibid.*, p. 57.
49. *Ibid.*, pp. 73-79.
50. *Ibid.*, pp. 80-85.
51. *Ibid.*, p. 99.
52. *Ibid.*, pp. 140-48.
53. *Ibid.*, p. 139.
54. *Ibid.*, pp. 153-54.
55. *Ibid.*, pp. 207-09.
56. Review of *Dog and Duck, Saturday Review,* CXXXVII (January-June, 1924), 391.
57. A. S. Godwin, "Correspondence," *Times Literary Supplement,* XXIII (March 13, 1924), 160.
58. Lady Benson, *Mainly Players,* p. 191.
59. St. John Adcock, *Modern Grub Street and Other Essays* (New York, n. d. 1928), pp. 14-15.
60. *Ibid.*, pp. 136-37.
61. *Ibid.*, pp. 137-38.
62. "Mr. Machen Serves Up a Literary Relish," *New York Times Book Review and Magazine* (February 10, 1924), p. 15.
63. *Works,* II, 180.
64. *Works,* IX, 77.
65. *Works,* III, 116-17.
66. *Ibid.*, p. 27.
67. *Ibid.*, p. 75.
68. *Ibid.*, pp. 165-67.
69. *Ibid.*, p. 154.
70. *Ibid.*, pp. 192-93.
71. *Ibid.*, p. 28.
72. *Ibid.*, pp. 98-101.
73. *Ibid.*, pp. 190-93, 243-45.
74. Annie Marble, *A Study of the Modern Novel* (New York, 1930), p. 51.
75. *Works,* III, 208.
76. Robert Hillyer, "Arthur Machen," *Yale Review,* XIII (October, 1923), 176.
77. *Works,* III, 8.
78. *Ibid.*, p. 19.
79. *Ibid.*, p. 207.
80. *Ibid.*, p. 122.

81. *Ibid.*, pp. 120-21.
82. *Ibid.*, p. 208.
83. Machen, Letter to Hillyer, September 4, 1924.
84. Machen, Letter to Hillyer, September 1, 1925.
85. Robert Hillyer, "Up from the Ranks of Grub Street Authorship," *New York Times Book Review and Magazine* (March 4, 1923), p. 21.
86. Cuthbert Wright, "Far-Off Things," *The Freeman*, VII (April 4, 1923), 91.
87. Hillyer, *op. cit.*, p. 5.
88. Robert Hillyer, "Reminiscences of Arthur Machen," *New York Times Book Review and Magazine* (November 5, 1922), p. 6.
89. *Ibid.*
90. Robert Hillyer, "Up from the Ranks of Grub Street Authorship," *New York Times Book Review and Magazine* (March 4, 1923), p. 5.
91. Machen, *Precious Balms*, p. 35.
92. Review of *The Hill of Dreams, Academy*, LXXII (March 16, 1907), 273-74.
93. Madeleine L. Cazamian, *L' Anti-Intellectualisme et L' Esthétisme: 1880-1900*, Vol. II of *Le Roman et Les Idées en Angleterre* (Paris, 1935), p. 260. My translation.
94. Machen, *The Cosy Room* (London, 1936), pp. 85-90.
95. *Ibid.*, p. 66.
96. John Gawsworth, *Strange Assembly* (London, 1932), p. 18.
97. Machen, "The Spagyric Quest of Beroaldus Cosmopolita," *Shining Pyramid* (Chicago, 1923), pp. 47-62.
98. Danielson, *op. cit.*, pp. 13-14.
99. Scarborough, *The Supernatural in Modern English Fiction*, pp. 139, 271.
100. *Ibid.*, p. 139.
101. A. E. Waite, *The Book of Black Magic* (London, 1898), p. 109.
102. Machen, Letter to Arnold Rubin, December 10, 1928.
103. *Works*, I, 51.
104. *Ibid.*, p. 81.
105. *Ibid.*, p. 13.
106. *Ibid.*
107. *Ibid.*, p. 20.
108. *Ibid.*, p. 29.
109. *Works*, V, 165-67.
110. Weygandt, *A Century of the English Novel*, p. 331.
111. Lovecraft, *Supernatural Horror in Literature*, p. 16.

112. Danielson, *op. cit.*, p. vi.
113. Machen, *Precious Balms,* pp. 1-19.
114. Rickett, *Lost Chords,* pp. 19-20.
115. Edmund Lester Pearson, "New Books and Old," *Independent,* CVIII (June 24, 1922), 558.
116. R. Ellis Roberts, "Arthur Machen," *Sewanee Review,* XXXII (July-September, 1924), 354-55.
117. Lovecraft, *op. cit.*, 89.
118. *Ibid.*, p. 15.
119. *Ibid.*, p. 12.
120. Fred J. Hando, *The Pleasant Land of Gwent* (Newport, Monmouthshire, 1944), p. 13.
121. *Letters,* p. 6.
122. *Anatomy,* p. 7.
123. Machen, *The Cosy Room,* p. 267.
124. William Francis Gekle, *Arthur Machen: Weaver of Fantasy* (Millbrook, New York, 1949), p. 55.
125. *Works,* V, 160.
126. *Works,* I, 19, 22, and 51.
127. Machen, *Great God Pan* (London, 1916), p. xviii.
128. Lovecraft, *op. cit.*, p. 92.
129. *Ibid.*
130. *Works,* II, 83.
131. *Ibid.*, pp. 89, 92, 95.
132. *Ibid.*, p. 101.
133. *Ibid.*, pp. 112, 114.
134. *Ibid.*, p. 182.
135. *Ibid.*, p. 165.
136. *Ibid.*, p. 173.
137. *Ibid.*, p. 177.
138. *Ibid.*, p. 173.
139. *Ibid.*, pp. 183-84.
140. *Ibid.*, p. 179.
141. *Ibid.*, p. 202.
142. *Ibid.*, p. 220.
143. Scarborough, *op. cit.*, p. 269.
144. Machen, *Tales of Horror and the Supernatural,* ed. Philip Van Doren Stern (New York, 1948), p. v. Reprinted by permission of Alfred A. Knopf, Inc.
145. "Novels," *Saturday Review,* CII (July 28, 1906), 117.
146. Carl Van Vechten, *Peter Whiffle* (New York, 1922), p. 200. All quotations reprinted by permission of Alfred A. Knopf, Inc.
147. "Novels," *Saturday Review,* CII (July 28, 1906), 117.

148. Starrett, *Buried Caesars*, p. 3.
149. Review of *The Three Impostors, New York Times Book Review and Magazine* (September 2, 1923), p. 22.
150. Basil Davenport, "The Devil Is Not Dead," *Saturday Review of Literature*, XIII (February 15, 1936), 4.
151. Scarborough, *op. cit.*, p. 73.
152. *Ibid.*, p. 117.
153. *Ibid.*, p. 247.
154. *Ibid.*, p. 250.
155. Bailey, *Pilgrims Through Time and Space*, p. 10.
156. *Ibid.*, p. 27.
157. *Ibid.*, pp. 191, 195, 198.
158. *Ibid.*, p. 198.
159. *Ibid.*, p. 212.
160. Albrecht, *op. cit.*, Chapter V.
161. Scarborough, *op. cit.*, p. 70.
162. Danielson, *op. cit.*, p. 27.
163. Scarborough, *op. cit.*, pp. 300-01.
164. Albrecht, *op. cit.*, p. 31.
165. Ernest Jones, "Tales of Arthur Machen," *Nation*, CLXVII (August 1, 1948), 190.
166. "Our Library Table," *Athenaeum*, II (August 4, 1906), 129.
167. Van Vechten, *Peter Whiffle*, pp. 196-97, 198-99, 200.
168. Ernest Jones, "Tales of Arthur Machen," *Nation*, CLXVII (August 1, 1948), 190.
169. Lovecraft, *op. cit.*, p. 92.
170. Basil Davenport, "The Devil Is Not Dead," *Saturday Review of Literature*, XIII (February 15, 1936), 4.
171. *Ibid.*
172. August Derleth, "A Note on Arthur Machen," *Reading and Collecting*, I (November, 1937), 6.
173. Scarborough, *op. cit.*, p. 79.
174. Machen, *House of Souls* (New York, 1923), p. xiv.
175. *Works*, VI, 123.
176. *Ibid.*, p. 131.
177. *Ibid.*, p. 127.
178. *Ibid.*, p. 128.
179. Davenport, *op. cit.*, p. 4.
180. *Works*, VI, 136, 137, 138, 143.
181. *Ibid.*, pp. 141, 144.
182. *Ibid.*, pp. 157-58.
183. *Ibid.*, pp. 146-48.
184. *Ibid.*, pp. 154-55.
185. *Ibid.*, pp. 161-67.

186. *Ibid.*, pp. 181-82.
187. Helen Lynch, "Arthur Machen," *Sewanee Review*, XLVII (July-September, 1939), 425.
188. Lovecraft, *op. cit.*, p. 91.
189. *Ibid.*, pp. 89-91.
190. Ben Hecht, "The Satyr—Machen: A Diagnosis of the Last Pagan," *Chicago Literary Times* (April 1, 1923), p. 3.
191. Machen, *The Angels of Mons*, 1st ed. (London, 1915), p. 13.
192. *Ibid.*, p. 18.
193. Harold Begbie, *On the Side of the Angels* (London, 1915), note and p. 9.
194. *Ibid.*, p. 19.
195. *Ibid.*, p. 126.
196. Ralph Shirley, *The Angel Warriors at Mons* (London, n. d.).
197. Machen, *The Angels of Mons*, 2nd ed. (London, 1915), p. 52.
198. *Works*, IX, 126.
199. Machen, *The Canning Wonder* (New York, 1926), pp. 16-17.
200. "The Angels of Mons," *New York Times Book Review*, XX (October 24, 1915), 406.
201. Scarborough, *op. cit.*, p. 204.
202. "Briefs on New Books," *Dial*, LIX (October 28, 1915), 382.
203. Machen, *The Angels of Mons*, 1st ed., pp. 21-23.
204. Albrecht, *op. cit.*, Chapter VII.
205. Daphne du Maurier, *Kiss Me Again, Stranger* (New York, 1953), pp. 32-66.
206. *Works*, VII, 47.
207. Jordan-Smith, *On Strange Altars*, p. 227.
208. "The Latest Works of Fiction," *New York Times Book Review*, XXII (October 14, 1917), 400.
209. *Works*, VII, 144.

Chapter Five

1. "Mr. Machen's Place Among Contemporary Writers," *Academy*, LXXIII (November 16, 1907), 148-49.
2. Machen, *Bridles & Spurs*, p. 21.
3. *Works*, VI, 126-27.
4. H. P. Lovecraft, "A Group of Letters," *Arkham Sampler*, I (Spring, 1948), 14, 15, 17. *Best Supernatural Stories* (Cleveland, 1945), pp. 147, 176, 218. *Supernatural Horror in Literature* (New York, 1945), pp. 85-95, 102, 106.
5. August Derleth, *H. P. L.: A Memoir* (New York, 1945), pp. 25, 67-68, 74, 75-76, 78.
6. Ray Bradbury, *The Illustrated Man* (New York, 1952), pp. 133, 137.

7. Henri Martineau, "Arthur Machen et P. J. Toulet," *Mercure de France,* CCLXXXI (January 1, 1938), 52.

8. Alfred Kazin, *On Native Grounds* (New York, 1942), pp. 169-70.

9. Douglas, *Autobiography,* p. 245.

Selected Bibliography

PRIMARY SOURCES

1. Books

In general, only first editions have been listed below in chronological order. However, since Machen wrote special introductions for some editions, these have been appended to the main entry wherever pertinent. In addition, the Caerleon edition of Machen's collected works has been inserted because it is a primary source for reference material in this study.

The Anatomy of Tobacco. London: George Redway, 1884. Also Carbonnek [New York]: [Boni and Liveright], 1923. Also London: Martin Secker, 1925. Also New York: Knopf, 1926.

The Chronicle of Clemendy. London: Privately printed, 1888. Also New York: Knopf, 1926.

The Great God Pan and the Inmost Light. London: John Lane, 1894. Also London: Simpkin, Marshall, Hamilton, Kent & Co., 1916.

The Three Impostors. London: John Lane, 1895. Also New York: Knopf, 1923.

The House of the Hidden Light. London: Privately printed, 1904.

The House of Souls. London: E. Grant Richards, 1906, 1923. Also New York: Knopf, 1923.

The Hill of Dreams. London: E. Grant Richards, 1907. Also New York: Knopf, 1923.

Dr. Stiggins: His Views and Principles. London: Francis Griffiths, 1906. Also New York: Knopf, 1925.

The Angels of Mons. 1st and 2nd eds. London: Simpkin, Marshall, Hamilton, Kent & Co., 1915.

The Great Return. London: The Faith Press, 1915.

The Terror. London: Duckworth & Co., 1917.

War and the Christian Faith. London: Skeffington & Son, 1918.

The Secret Glory. London: Martin Secker, 1922. Also New York: Knopf, 1922.

Far Off Things. London: Martin Secker, 1922.

Caerleon Edition of the Works. 9 vols. London: Martin Secker, 1923.

Things Near & Far. London: Martin Secker, 1923.
The Shining Pyramid. Chicago: Covici-McGee, 1923.
Strange Roads. London: The Classic Press, 1923.
Dog and Duck. New York: Knopf, 1924.
The London Adventure or the Art of Wandering. London: Martin Secker, 1924. Also New York: Knopf, 1924.
The Glorious Mystery. Chicago: Covici-McGee, 1924.
Precious Balms. London: Spurr & Swift, 1924.
Ornaments in Jade. New York: Knopf, 1924.
The Shining Pyramid. London: Martin Secker, 1925. Contents differ from 1923 edition.
The Canning Wonder. London: Chatto & Windus, 1925.
Dreads and Drolls. London: Martin Secker, 1926.
Notes and Queries. London: Spurr & Swift, 1926.
Tom O' Bedlam and His Song. Westport, Conn.: The Apellicon Press, 1930.
A Few Letters from Arthur Machen. Cleveland: The Rowfant Club, 1932.
The Green Round. London: Ernest Benn, 1933.
The Cosy Room. London: Rich & Cowan, 1936.
The Children of the Pool. London: Hutchinson & Co., 1936.
Bridles & Spurs. Cleveland: The Rowfant Club, 1951.

2. Pamphlets

Only those pamphlets are listed which contain original material by Machen not easily found in print elsewhere.

Eleusinia. Hereford, Wales: Privately printed, 1881.
The Grande Trouvaille. London: The First Edition Bookshop, 1923.
A Souvenir of Cadby Hall. London: J. Lyons & Co., 1927.
Beneath the Barley A Note on the Origins of Eleusinia. London: Privately printed, 1931.
In the 'Eighties. Amersham: Privately printed, 1931.

3. Translations

Other than first editions, only those are listed which have a new introduction by Machen.

Marguerite, Queen of Navarre. *The Heptameron*. London: Dryden Press, 1886. Also New York: Knopf, 1924.
De Verville, Beroalde. *Fantastic Tales*. London: Privately printed, 1890. Also New York: Boni & Liveright, 1923.
Casanova, Jacques. *The Memoirs of Jacques Casanova*. London: Pri-

vately printed, 1894. *The Memoirs of Giacomo Casanova Di Seingalt.* London: Casanova Society, 1922. *The Memoirs of Jacques Casanova De Seingalt.* New York: Aventuros, 1925. Also Edinburgh: Limited Editions Club, 1940.

Casanova, Jacques. *Casanova's Escape from the Leads.* London: Casanova Society, 1925. Also New York: Knopf, 1925.

Stanhope, Lady Hester Lucy. *Remarks upon Hermodactylus.* London: Privately printed, 1933.

4. Prefaces

The entries from this point on are alphabetical rather than chronological.

Benson, Lady Constance. *Mainly Players: Bensonian Memories.* London: Thornton Butterworth, 1926.

Brillat-Savarin, J. A. *The Physiology of Taste.* London: Peter Davies, 1925.

Brunelli, Bruno. *Casanova Loved Her.* London: Peter Davies, 1929.

Buck, Mitchell S. *Afterglow: Pastels of Greek Egypt 69 B.C.* New York: Nicholas L. Brown, 1924.

Carter, Frederick. *The Dragon of the Alchemists.* London: Elkin Mathews, 1926.

Cheng, F. T. *Civilization and the Art of China.* London: William Clowes & Sons, 1936.

Collins, William J. T., ed. *The Romance of the Echoing Wood.* Newport, Monmouthshire: R. H. Johns, 1937.

Dewar, George A. B. *The Pageant of English Landscape.* London: The Classic Press, 1924.

Douglas, Robert B., trans. *One Hundred Merrie & Delightsome Stories.* New York: Boni and Liveright, 1924.

Gawsworth, John. *Above the River.* London: Ulysses Bookshop, 1931.

Greenwood, Edwin. *Skin and Bone.* London: Skeffington & Son, 1934.

Hando, Fred J. *The Pleasant Land of Gwent.* Newport, Monmouthshire: R. H. Johns, 1944.

A Handy Dickens. London: Constable & Co., 1941.

Hillyer, Robert. *The Halt in the Garden.* London: Elkin Mathews, 1925.

Hudleston, Francis J. *Gentleman Johnny Burgoyne.* London: Jonathan Cape, 1928.

Middleton, Richard Barham. *The Ghost Ship & Other Stories.* London: T. Fisher Unwin, 1912.

Miró, Gabriel. *Our Father San Daniel,* trans. Charlotte Remfry-Kidd. London: Ernest Benn, 1930.

Sergeant, Philip W. *Witches and Warlocks.* London: Hutchinson, 1936.

Smollett, Tobias. *The Expedition of Humphry Clinker.* New York: The Modern Library, 1929.

Stonor, Oliver, trans. *The Way to Succeed.* France: Hesperides Press, 1930.

5. Anthologies

Machen's tales and essays have been reproduced in dozens of anthologies. The ones listed below contain works that have not been located elsewhere. Machen's work follows the main entry in quotation marks. Books containing letters by Machen have been omitted.

Asquith, Cynthia, ed. *The Treasure Cave.* London: Jarrolds, 1928. "Johnny Double."

Keating, George T., Collection of. *A Conrad Memorial Library.* New York: Doubleday, Doran & Company, 1929. "Victory."

Missing from Their Homes. London: Hutchinson, 1936. "The Dover Road."

Pope, T. Michael, ed. *The Book of Fleet Street.* London: Cassell and Company, 1930. "The Ready Reporter."

Rowland, John, ed. *Path and Pavement.* London: Eric Grant, 1937. "Ritual."

Saintsbury, H. A., and Cecil Palmer, eds. *We Saw Him Act.* London: Hurst & Blackett, 1939. "Irving as Don Quixote."

Starrett, Vincent, ed. *Et Cetera, a Collector's Scrapbook.* Chicago: Pascal Covici, 1924. "English and Irish" and "My Murderer."

Turner, Walter J., ed. *Great Names.* New York: The Dial Press, 1926. "Sir Walter Scott."

6. Periodicals

Machen made his living for long periods by writing for newspapers and magazines. These entries alone would fill approximately one hundred printed pages. Only the names of periodicals which contain numerous contributions appear below, along with inclusive dates. His better tales and essays have been reprinted in book form.

The Academy, 1907-1908.
The Academy and Literature, 1910-1912.
The Daily Mail, 1909-1910.
The Evening News, 1910-1921.
The Independent, 1933-1935.
John O'London's Weekly, 1919-1940.

Literature, 1898-1899.
The London Graphic, 1925-1926.
The Lyons Mail, 1919-1923.
The Observer, 1926-1937.
St. James's Gazette, 1889-1890.
The Sunday Express, 1928-1929.
The Sunday Times, 1921-1939.
T. P.'s and Cassell's Weekly, 1923-1928.
T. P.'s Weekly, 1908-1915.
Vanity Fair, 1907.
Walford's Antiquarian, 1887.

SECONDARY SOURCES

Only major sources of biographical, bibliographical, and critical information have been listed below. Numerous other sources for random facts can be found in Notes and References.

Adcock, St. John. *The Glory That Was Grub Street.* New York: Frederick A. Stokes Company (n. d. 1928). Contains reminiscences by a fellow hack writer of Machen's activities prior to World War I, particularly the clubs to which he belonged.

Albrecht, W. P. "Arthur Machen: A Critical Study." Unpublished dissertation. University of Pittsburgh, 1934. A balanced but incomplete study based only on major works.

Brown, W. Sorley. *The Life and Genius of T. W. H. Crosland.* London: Cecil Palmer, 1928. Machen's testimony at a law suit indicating his strong Anglo-Catholic position.

Cabell, James Branch. *Beyond Life.* New York: Robert H. McBride & Company, 1919. An attempt to overcome the neglect of Machen's work through a stirring tribute to his genius.

Carrington, Hereward. *Psychical Phenomena and the War.* New York: Dodd, Mead and Company, 1918. Historical study placing the legend created by *The Angels of Mons* in proper perspective.

Cazamian, Madeleine L. *L' Anti-Intellectualisme et L' Esthétisme: 1880-1900,* vol. II of *Le Roman et Les Idées en Angleterre.* Paris: Les Belles Lettres, 1935. The most scholarly and perceptive study of Machen's relationship to other writers of the 1890's.

Childs, J. Rives. *Casanoviana.* Vienna: Christian M. Nebehay, 1956. A bibliography of Casanova's *Memoirs* listing all publications of the Machen translation up to 1956 as a part of the study.

Clarence, O. B. *No Complaints.* London: Jonathan Cape, 1943. Memoirs of acting including days with the Benson Company and anecdotes about Machen.

Clark, Emily. *Innocence Abroad.* New York: Alfred A. Knopf, 1931.

An account of *The Reviewer* mentioning Machen's connection with it and some details of his Dog and Duck parties of the 1920's.

Cumberland, Gerald. *Written in Friendship*. London: Grant Richards, Ltd., 1923. Describes Machen during his days as a reporter.

Danielson, Henry. *Arthur Machen A Bibliography*. London: Henry Danielson, 1923. An incomplete bibliography which has interesting notes written by Machen on his early works.

Douglas, Lord Alfred Bruce. *The Autobiography of Lord Alfred Douglas*. London: Martin Secker, 1929. Contains a one-sided view of Douglas's association with Machen during *The Academy* period and of Machen's later "ingratitude."

Ellis, Stewart M. *Mainly Victorian*. London: Hutchinson & Co., (n. d. 1925). A collection of essays written by an acquaintance of Machen containing some reminiscences and one critical essay on Machen's works.

Gekle, William Francis. *Arthur Machen: Weaver of Fantasy*. Millbrook, New York: Round Table Press, 1949. A book of enthusiasms on Machen's works; contains a worthwhile bibliography.

Goldstone, Adrian and Wesley Sweetser. *A Bibliography of Arthur Machen*. Austin: University of Texas Press, 1964. The definitive work.

Gunther, John. "The Truth About Arthur Machen," *The Bookman,* LXI (July, 1925), 571-74. A revealing interview with Machen during his heyday by a now-prominent writer.

Hecht, Ben. "Arthur Machen," *The Chicago Daily News* (November 7, 1917), 12. An account by a one-time acquaintance whose literary views did not coincide with those of Machen.

Hillyer, Robert. "Arthur Machen," *The Atlantic,* CLXXIX (May, 1947), 138-40. A personal reminiscence of a common experience written by a long-time friend. "Up from the Ranks of Grub Street Authorship," *The New York Times Book Review and Magazine* (March 4, 1923), 5, 21. A valuable critique of Machen's works. "Arthur Machen," *Yale Review,* XIII (October, 1923), 174-76. A sound review of *Things Near & Far* and *The Hill of Dreams* showing Machen's mystic and humanistic qualities.

Hind, C. Lewis. *More Authors and I*. New York: Dodd, Mead and Company, 1922. A recollection of a meeting with Machen during *The Evening News* days with some commentary on Machen's works.

Hinton, Percival. "Arthur Machen: A Note," *The Amateur Book Collector,* III (November, 1952), 2. Machen's works from the collector's point of view.

Jepson, Edgar. *Memories of an Edwardian and Neo-Georgian.* London: Richards, 1937. Accurate facts on Machen's life during the early twentieth century, written by an old friend. Includes the minutes of the New Bohemians Club and a postscript written by Machen.

Jerome, Jerome K. *My Life and Times.* London: Hodder and Stoughton, Ltd., (n. d. 1926). One of the few sources of information on Machen's first wife.

Jordan-Smith, Paul. "A Little Journey to the Home of Arthur Machen," *The Wave,* I (June, 1922), 35-37. Personal account of St. John's Wood by an American collector of Machen's works.

———. *For the Love of Books.* New York: Oxford University Press, 1934. The best account of the difficulties in collecting Machen's books.

———. *On Strange Altars.* New York: Albert & Charles Boni, 1924. A balanced though brief analysis of Machen's major works with some personal anecdotes.

Kunitz, Stanley J. and Howard Haycraft, eds. *Twentieth Century Authors.* New York: H. W. Wilson Company, 1942. Brief, inaccurate life.

Lejeune, Anthony. "An Old Man and a Boy: Memories of Arthur Machen," *The Listener,* LV (March 29, 1956), 315, 318-19. Vignette of Machen at Amersham.

Lovecraft, H. P. *The Outsider and Others.* Sauk City, Wis.: Arkham House, 1939. Outstanding study of supernatural horror placing Machen in proper perspective in that genre, written by a master in the same field who was much influenced by Machen.

Mais, S. P. B. *Some Modern Authors.* London: Grant Richards, Ltd., 1923. A tribute from a friend.

Michael, D. P. M. "The Life and Works of Arthur Machen with Special Reference to His Novels and Tales." Unpublished dissertation. University of Wales, 1941. Authoritative facts of the life acquired by correspondence with Machen, but inadequate critique.

Morrissey, Ralph Grainger. "Arthur Machen: A Study." Unpublished dissertation. Vanderbilt University, 1930. A thesis containing unpublished correspondence with Machen.

Peterley, David. *Peterley Harvest.* London: Hutchinson of London, 1960. Memoirs containing some Machen correspondence and some recollections of Amersham.

Redway, George. "Some Reminiscences of Publishing Fifty Years Ago," *The Bookman,* LXXXI (December, 1931), 186-87. Only secondary source concerning Machen's work in the 1880's.

Reynolds, Aidan and William Charlton. *Arthur Machen.* London: The

Richards Press, 1963. A short account of his life and a few of the major works.

Roberts, R. Ellis. "Arthur Machen," *The Bookman,* LXII (September, 1922), 240-42. A sound critique covering many of the major works.

Savage, Henry. "Arthur Machen: A Personal Sketch of the Famous Writer," *Book Notes,* I (August-September, 1923), 143-44, 164. By Machen's long-time literary agent.

Scarborough, Dorothy. *The Supernatural in Modern English Fiction.* New York: G. P. Putnam's Sons, 1917. By far the best, most inclusive study of Machen's relative position in the field of the supernatural.

Sewell, Father Brocard, ed. *Arthur Machen.* Llandeilo, Wales: St. Albert's Press, 1960. A collection of essays, one by the present author and several by persons who knew Machen.

Shiel, M. P. *The Borzoi 1925.* New York: Alfred A. Knopf, 1925. A chapter on Machen by a fellow writer of fantasy and an old acquaintance.

Starrett, Vincent. *Buried Caesars.* Chicago: Covici-McGee, 1923. Adulation by the writer most responsible for Machen's recognition in America during the 1920's.

Sweetser, Wesley D. "The Works of Arthur Machen: An Analysis and Bibliography." Unpublished doctoral dissertation. University of Colorado, 1958. The most complete life and critique thus far.

Tante, Dilly, ed. *Living Authors.* New York: H. W. Wilson Company, 1931. A useful short life.

van Patten, Nathan. "James Branch Cabell and Arthur Machen," *The Hesperian* (Summer, 1930), 23-25. An interesting comparison.

Van Vechten, Carl. *Peter Whiffle: His Life and Works.* New York: Alfred A. Knopf, 1922. Enthusiasms by one of Machen's early American discoverers.

———. *Excavations.* New York: Alfred A. Knopf, 1926. A balanced critique of the major works.

Wagenknecht, Edward. *Cavalcade of the English Novel.* New York: Henry Holt and Company, 1943. A survey by a distinguished scholar and an admirer of Machen's work showing his relative insignificance in this field.

Waite, Arthur Edward. *Shadows of Life and Thought.* London: Selwyn and Blount, 1938. Biographical reminiscences by Machen's oldest friend.

Walzer, Pierre-Olivier. *Paul-Jean Toulet: L' œuvre L' écrivain.* Paris: Editions Des Portes de France, 1949. A study showing Machen's influence on Toulet.

Wells, Geoffrey H. "A Welsh Border Writer," *The Welsh Outlook* (January, 1924), 15-16. A view of Machen's Welsh background.

Weygandt, Cornelius. *A Century of the English Novel.* New York: The Century Co., 1925. Unfavorable comment on Machen as a novelist.

Index